BREAKING DOWN THE WALL

Between Americans and
East Germans—
Jews and Christians
Through Dialogue

Edited by

Leonard Swidler

LESTER DEAN   STEFAN SCHREINER
LEWIS ERON   LEONARD SWIDLER
ALAN MITTLEMAN   WERNER VOGLER
      JOHANNES HILDEBRANDT

UNIVERSITY
PRESS OF
AMERICA

LANHAM • NEW YORK • LONDON

Copyright © 1987 by

University Press of America,® Inc.

4720 Boston Way
Lanham, MD 20706

3 Henrietta Street
London WC2E 8LU England

British Cataloging in Publication Information Available

Library of Congress Cataloging-in-Publication Data

"Breaking down the wall" between Americans and East
Germans—Jews and Christians through dialogue.

Bibliography: p.
1. Judaism—Relations—Christianity—1945-
Congresses. 2. Christianity and other religions—
Judiasm—1945-   —Congresses. I. Swidler,
Leonard J.
BM535.B68   1987   261.2'6   87-2159
ISBN 0-8191-6176-4 (alk. paper)
ISBN 0-8191-6177-2 (pbk. : alk. paper)

All University Press of America books are produced on acid-free
paper which exceeds the minimum standards set by the National
Historical Publication and Records Commission.

CONTENTS

AMERICANS AND EAST GERMANS--JEWS AND CHRISTIANS: A DIALOGUE

Nine Americans from the Religion Department of Temple University, Philadelphia, Pennsylvania, went to East Germany in early May, 1984, for two weeks of dialogue with the faculties and the students of Protestant theological seminaries. The topic was Jewish-Christian dialogue. The American delegation consisted of two professors and seven advanced doctoral students--five Jews and four Christians, Catholic and Protestant. Three were women, and six were men; there were three rabbis, one rabbinical student (a woman), one Lutheran pastor, and four lay people.

This dialogue journey grew out of a similar experience four years earlier when four Temple University Religions Department faculty and thirteen advanced doctoral students engaged in a year-long seminar of Jewish-Christian dialogue in parallel with similar seminars in nine West German universities, culminating in an eight-week journey around West Germany for face-to-face dialogues after the "paper" dialogue. At that time invitations were forthcoming from East Germany, but visas were not. Two more attempts to obtain the requisite visas were made in the ensuing years, but success was attained only after much correspondence and many visits to East Berlin by myself and, most of all, by the "thaw" that developed during the "Luther Year" in 1983.

An official invitation was issued by the ecumenical office of the Protestant Church in East Germany, with offices in East Berlin. The initial efforts over the years on the East German side had been undertaken by Pastor Johannes Hildebrandt of East Berlin, and the final arrangements were handled by Oberkirchenrat Helmut Tschoerner of East Berlin. Arrangements were made for the American delegation to visit the faculty and students at the Protestant theological seminaries in East Berlin and Leipzig. Efforts to involve the Catholic theological faculty at Erfurt did not succeed (though they did on a later dialogue trip in 1986).

The fundamental reason why the East German Protestants were interested in such an exchange is that some of them are well aware of the creative work that has been going on in Western Germany and America in recent years in the field of Jewish-Christian dialogue. They were convinced that this is both a vital concern

1

for Christians in general and for Christian theology, and also especially for German Christians in light of the Holocaust of the Jews by Nazi Germany. However, there is very little that they are able to do about this concern on their own since there is no flourishing Jewish community left in East Germany. There are fewer than 500 practicing Jews in all of East Germany, and they do not have even a single rabbi. Hence, there are almost no partners with whom Christians in East Germany can conduct a Jewish-Christian dialogue. Since the Religion Department at Temple University is known for its interreligious dialogue structure and program, especially Jewish-Christian dialogue, it was invited to send a team of faculty and advanced students to share this expertise with the East Germans on both a scholarly and an experiential level.

The funding for this undertaking came from four sources: (1) the Protestant Church in East Germany, which provided the American delegation with its food, lodging, entertainment, and travel for two weeks that it was in East Germany; (2) the International Research and Exchanges Board (IREX) provided travel expenses for some of the delegation; (3) the American Jewish Committee also provided travel expenses for some of the American delegation; (4) honoraria resulting from lectures given by members of the delegation at various Catholic and Protestant academies, church groups, universities, a Jewish center, and the like in West Germany both immediately before and after the two-week stay in East Germany.

The American delegation went first to East Berlin where it stayed for several days at the East Berlin Protestant theological seminary, known as the Sprachenkonvikt. Each of the nine members of the American delegation had carefully prepared a scholarly paper during the previous academic year, and each had an opportunity to deliver his or her paper and have it discussed by the faculty and the students of the seminary. Several East German faculty members also delivered appropriate papers, which were discussed.

Through some previous confusion the seminary officials apparently thought that the American delegation was to meet only with the faculty. Fortunately, this began to change as soon as the first session was held. By the time of the second session, almost the entire student body (approximately 90) began to attend and participate in all the sessions. The interaction with

2

the faculty and especially the students would have to be described as superb. At the end of the week's stay at the East Berlin seminary, one of the East Berlin professors--in making a formal set of closing remarks--stated that, "We were supposed to host the Americans, but in fact it was the Americans who hosted us!", to which there were loud cheers on the part of all the faculty and students.

There was also contact with the faculty and students of the theological faculty at the Humboldt University in East Berlin. Several of the Americans visited the chairperson of the theological faculty, Professor Heinrich Fink, both at his office and at his home, and a number of that faculty and student body attended the sessions at the theological seminary.

Direct contact was also taken up with the Jewish community in East Berlin which, though extremely small, is nevertheless the largest by far in all of East Germany. Visits by the American delegation and faculty and students from the Protestant seminary were made to the ruins of the famous synagogue in East Berlin and the present offices of the Jewish community where a reception and dialogue were held, and also to both the large Jewish cemetery in East Berlin and the one intact large synagogue. At this latter, an explanatory tour was conducted, and synagogue services were held for the entire student body of the seminary.

The atmosphere that was quickly generated was so open and intense that after one day everyone from the American delegation and scores of the East Germans reached an emotional high which doubtless not only left indelible psychic marks on all concerned, but also sparked many personal friendships.

The American delegation then took the train to Leipzig where it had a very similar experience. There, too, it met with the local Jewish community (which in the last eight years had shrunk from 140 to 46!). Since they were there over the weekend, Professor Rabbi Zalman Schachter of the American delegation along with the President of the local community conducted Sabbath services, which were also attended by a large number of Christian faculty and students. Needless to say, the Leipzig Jewish community, small and fast disappearing but nevertheless proud and deterined to live Jewishly until the end, was overjoyed at the presence of the Jewish visitors, especially so many rabbis and young

3

people. The woman Jewish rabbinical student, Joanna Katz, became the center of special attention and affection for the women of the Leipzig Jewish community--for obvious reasons.

While at Leipzig the American delegation was taken on a one-day trip to visit Wittenberg (after the 1983 Luther Year, now called "Lutherstadt Wittenberg"). The high point of the visit to Wittenberg was the Preachers Seminary, a Protestant Church institution that works with young Protestant pastors after they have entered into pastoral work. The American delegation was extremely impressed by the spirit and method used at this institution, and the director was also extremely open to the contribution of Jewish-Christian dialogue to his work--so much so, that he invited Professor Rabbi Zalman Schachter to join his faculty on a visiting basis.

As in East Berlin, the American delegation delivered its several papers and had them discussed with the faculty and student body, and several members of the Leipzig theological faculty did the same. Again, the rapport that was generated between the American delegation and the East German faculty and student body was extraordinarily positive and warm, and many new friends were made.

At the end of the visit to Leipzig the American delegation went for a one-day visit to the city of Dresden, where it also met with members of the local Jewish community. Then it returned to East Berlin where there was a farewell dinner given by Oberkirchenrat Tschoerner and his staff members who had worked so long to make this dialogue journey the creative reality that it became.

The American delegation then crossed over into West Berlin where it stayed for some three days and engaged in Jewish-Christian dialogues of various sorts for six different institutions: the Catholic Academy, the Protestant Academy, the Jewish Community Center, the Protestant Theological Institute of Higher Learning, the Theological Faculty of the Free University, and a Protestant congregation. In addition to this, the American delegation had also conducted a weekend conference with a number of lectures and dialogues at the Catholic Academy of Münster, as well as a lecture by Professor Leonard Swidler at the

4

Protestant Theological Faculty of the University of Hamburg.

Just before the Americans left East Berlin, Oberkirchenrat Tschoerner related that he had had nothing but the most positive reports from all sources concerning the seminar and that he himself felt the same way. Moreover, he hoped that something similar would again be possible in the not too distant future. (In fact, an even more extensive dialogue seminar took place in March, 1986.)

In a project involving persons with widely differing knowledge concerning the topics involved, i.e., Christianity in the U.S. and East Germany and Jewish-Christian dialgoue, a certain amount of survey work had to be presented. These tasks were indispensable for the dialogues; they would not, however, make appropriate inclusions in a book bringing together the papers making a contribution to Jewish-Christian dialogue scholarship, as this volume intends. Nevertheless, because each member of the American delegation made her or his own special contribution which helped turn this dialogue seminar into a profound journey of the human spirit for each of the Americans and many of the Germans, the names of all should be recorded here: Ronald Bagnal, Lester Dean, Lewis Eron, Joanna Katz, Alan Mittleman, Carla Paap, Zalman Schachter, Brigid Shea, Leonard Swidler.

Most of the essays in this volume were originally lectures delivered in German within the context of the Jewish-Christian dialogue seminar in either Berlin or Leipzig. They have been somewhat revised for publication. The essay "Germany, Christianity and the Jews: From Diatribe to Dialogue" provides a general context within which Jewish-Christian dialogue in contemporary Germany takes place. The brief report on grass-roots Jewish-Christian dialogue by Pastor Johannes Hildebrandt systematically describes on paper his year-around Jewish-Christian dialogue activity--which the Americans experienced first-hand for the two weeks he was with them.

Three of the authors are Jewish and four Christian--three Protestant and one Catholic. Two of the essays offer reasons why Jewish-Christian dialogue can and should take place, one from a Christian perspective and the other from a Jewish one; both break new ground. Three essays survey descriptively the recent course of Jewish-Christian dialogue in Germany, and three focus on different aspects of the splintering point, when Judaism and Christianity divided and developed in their separate ways in the first century of the Common Era.

Each of these essays, in different ways, begins to build a bridge to the other side of the gulf of diatribe, the fundaments of which are critical scholarship and dialogue.

Leonard Swidler

THE PARADIGM SHIFT AND ITS IMPLICATIONS
FOR INTERRELIGIOUS DIALOGUE

Interreligious and Interideological Dialogue:
The Matrix for All Systematic Reflection Today

by

Leonard Swidler

If a complex reality is to be understood, the various parts and their interrelationships must be perceived within the context of a certain pattern, model, or paradigm: e.g., the sun, moon and planets do what they do because they circle around the earth; or, the earth, moon and other planets do what they do because they circle around the sun. Whether one chooses a geocentric or a heliocentric paradigm makes a considerable difference in how one understands the cosmos.

We are living today in the West, and elsewhere, in the midst of a massive paradigm shift in our understanding of understanding, which fundamentally affects our whole perception of reality and its meaning--another word for which is "religion," the "explanation of the meaning of life and how to live accordingly." As the paradigm shift in our understanding of understanding, of truth statements, proceeds, the traditional absolutisms of the religions and ideologies are being replaced with more pluralistic, dialogic understandings of the meaning of reality and the way to live accordingly. The appropriate stance of one religion or ideology toward others, then, is no longer being seen as that of imperialism or indifference, but interreligious, interideological dialogue.

Therefore, I want to argue that interreligious and interideological dialogue is the most appropriate matrix within which all thinkers ought to carry out their systematic reflections on their explanations of the meaning of life and how to live accordingly--called by Christians, theology. (Most explanations of the meaning of life and how to live accordingly have in the past entailed a belief in a divinity--Theravada Buddhism is a clear exception--and in recent centuries have been called by the West, religions. Those most recent explanations of the meaning of life and how to live accordingly which do not include a belief in a divinity, for example, Marxism, have at times been

7

called ideologies. I am here adopting that terminology.)

After a description of what is meant by dialogue,
I will describe briefly the recent process of deabsolutizing our understanding of truth and how this has
led to the possibility and necessity of dialogue;
applying this fact to theology and other systematic
reflections leads to the need for interreligious,
interideological dialogue, for which I will outline
some necessary groundrules. But how to carry out
interreligious, interideological dialogue? This will
be the heart of this essay: an attempt to show the way
forward, not in the "practical" and depth or
"spiritual" areas (each of them warrants separate, full
treatment), but in the "cognitive" area by way of
"ecumenical Esperanto." The conclusion will be that
the new relational, dialogical paradigm through which
we understand reality is advancing in all areas of
knowledge, including this most comprehensive area of
making sense out of the whole of life. Hence, no
systematic reflection on the "meaning of life and how
to live accordingly" can appropriately be done outside
of the matrix of interreligious, interideological
dialogue.

I. DIALOGUE

Dialogue of course is conversation between two or
more persons with differing views, the primary purpose
of which is for each participant to learn from the
other so that he or she can change and grow. Minimally
the very fact that I learn that my dialogue partner
believes "this," rather than "that," proportionally
changes my attitude toward her; and a change in my
attitude is a significant change, and growth, in me.
We enter into dialogue, therefore, so that we can
learn, change and grow, not so that we can force change
on the other. In the past when encountering those who
differed with us in the religious and ideological
sphere we did so usually either to defeat them as an
opponent, or to learn about them so as to more effectively deal with them. In other words, we usually
faced those who differed with us as in confrontation--
sometimes more openly polemically, sometimes more
subtly so, but usually with the ultimate goal of over-
coming the other because we were convinced that we
alone had the truth.

8

But that is not what dialogue is. Dialogue is not debate. In dialogue each partner must listen to the other as openly and sympathetically as he or she can in an attempt to understand the other's position as precisely and, as it were, as much from within, as possible. Such an attitude automatically includes the assumption that at any point we might find the partner's position so persuasive that, if we would act with integrity, we would have to change.

Until quite recently in almost all religious traditions, and certainly very definitely within Christianity, the idea of seeking religious, ideological wisdom, insight, truth, by way of dialogue, other than in a very initial, rudimentary fashion, occurred to very few people, and certainly had no influence in the major religious or ideological communities. The further idea of pursuing religious or ideological truth through dialogue between differing religions and ideologies was even more unheard of (if one can speak thus!). For example, it was merely a century and a half ago that Pope Gregory XVI penned those fateful lines: "We come now to a source which is, alas! all too productive of the deplorable evils afflicting the Church today. We have in mind indifferentism, that is, the fatal opinion everywhere spread abroad by the deceit of wicked men, that the eternal salvation of the soul can be won by the profession of any faith at all, provided that conduct conforms to the norms of justice and probity. . . . From this poisonous spring of indifferentism flows the false and absurd, or rather the mad principle (deliramentum) that we must secure and guarantee to each one liberty of conscience."[1] Not only was dialogue with the other disallowed, so was even being other!

Today the situation is dramatically reversed. No less a person than Pope Paul VI in 1964 in his very first encyclical focused on dialogue, stating that "dialogue is demanded nowadays. . . . is demanded by the dynamic course of action which is changing the face of modern society. It is demanded by the pluralism of society and by the maturity man has reached in this day and age. Be he religious or not, his secular education has enabled him to think and speak, and to conduct dialogue with dignity."[2] We hear many more official words of encouragement from the Vatican secretariat for dialogue with atheists: "All Christians should do their best to promote dialogue . . . as a duty of fraternal charity suited to our progressive and adult

9

age." Further, "the willingness to engage in dialogue is the measure and strength of that general renewal which must be carried out in the Church." Moreover, this dialogue is not thought of solely in terms of "practial" matters, but in a central way is to focus on theology and doctrine and to do so without hesitation or trepidation: "Doctrinal dialogue should be initiated with courage and sincerity, with the greatest of freedom and with reverence. It focuses on doctrinal questions which are of concern to the parties in dialogue. They have different opinions but by common effort they strive to improve mutual understanding, to clarify matters on which they agree, and if possible to enlarge the areas of agreement. In this way the parties to dialogue can enrich each other."[3]

II. DEABSOLUTIZING TRUTH

Why this dramatic change? Why, indeed, should one pursue the truth in the areas of religion and ideology by way of dialogue? A fundamental answer to these questions lies in the even more dramatic shift in the understanding of truth that has taken place first in Western civilization, and now beyond, throughout the nineteenth and twentieth centuries, making dialogue not only possible but also necessary.

Whereas before the notion of truth was largely absolute, static, and exclusive up to the last century, it has subsequently become deabsolutized, dynamic and dialogic--in a word, "relational." This new view of truth came about in at least four different, but closely related, ways. I will list and then briefly describe each.

1. Historicizing of truth: truth is deabsolutized and dynamized in terms of time, both past and future, with intentionality and action playing a major role in the latter.

2. Sociology of knowledge: truth is deabsolutized in terms of geography, culture and social standing.

3. Limitations of language: truth as the meaning of something and especially as talk about the transcendent is deabsolutized by the nature of human language.

10

4. Hermeneutics: all truth, all knowledge is seen as interpreted truth, knowledge, and hence is deabsolutized by the observer who always is also interpreter.

1. The historicizing of truth: Before the nineteenth century in Europe truth, that is, a statement about reality, was conceived in quite an absolute, static, exclusivistic either-or manner. It was thought that if something was true at some time or other, it was always true, and not only in the sense of empirical facts but also in the sense of the meaning of things or the oughtness that was said to flow from them. For example, if is was true for the Pauline writer to say in the first century that women should keep silence in the church, then it was always true that women should keep silence in the church; or if it was true for Pope Boniface VIII in 1302 to state in definitive terms that "we declare, state, and define that it is absolutely necessary for the salvation of all human beings that they submit to the Roman Pontiff," then it was always true that they need do so. At bottom the notion of truth was based on the Aristotlian principle of contradiction: a thing could not be true and not true in the same way at the same time. Truth was defined by way of exclusion; A was A because it could be shown not to be not-A. Truth was thus understood to be absolute, static, exclusivistically either-or. This is a classicist or absolutist view of truth.

In the nineteenth century many scholars came to perceive all statements about the truth of the meaning of something as being partially products of their historical circumstances. Those concrete circumstances helped determine the fact that the statement under study was even called forth, that it was couched in particular intellectual categories (for example, abstract Platonic, or concrete legal language), particular literary forms (for example, mythic, or metaphysical language), and particular psychological settings (for example, a polemic response to a specific attack). It was argued by these scholars that only by placing the truth statements in their historical situation, their historical Sitz im Leben, could they be properly understood (understanding of the text could be found only in context), and that to express the same original meaning in a later Sitz im Leben one would require a proportionately different statement. Thus, all statements about the meaning of things were seen to be deab-

11

solutized in terms of time. This is a historical view of truth. Clearly at its heart is a notion of relationality, namely, a statement about the truth of the meaning of something has to be understood in relationship to its historical context.

Later, especially with the work of thinkers like Max Scheler and Karl Mannheim, a corollary was added to this historicizing of knowledge; it concerned not the past but the future. These and other scholars also conceived of the knowledge of truth as having an element of intentionality at the base of it, as being oriented ultimately toward action, praxis. They argued that we perceive certain things as questions to be answered and set goals to pursue certain knowledge because we wish to do something about those matters; we intend to live according to the truth, the meaning of things, that we hope to discern in the answering of the questions we pose, in gaining the knowledge we decide to seek. Thus, the truth of the meaning of things as stated by anyone was seen as deabsolutized by the action-oriented intentionality of the thinker-speaker. This is a praxis view of truth, and it too is basically relational, that is, a statement had to be understood in relationship to the action-oriented intention of the speaker.

2. The sociology of knowledge: As the statements of the truth about the meaning of things were seen by some thinkers to be historically deabsolutized in time, so also starting in this century such statements were seen to be deabsolutized by the cultural, class (and so forth) standpoint of the thinker-speaker, regardless of time. Thus, a statement about the true meaning of things will be partially determined by the worldview of the thinker-speaker. All reality was said to be perceived from the cultural, class, sexual (and so forth) perspective of the perceiver. Therefore, any statement of the truth of the meaning of something was seen to be perspectival, "standpoint-bound," standortgebunden, as Karl Mannheim put it, and thus deabsolutized. This is a perspectival view of truth, which is likewise relational, for all statements are fundamentally related to the standpoint of the speaker.

3. The limitations of language: Many thinkers (following Ludwig Wittgenstein and others) have come to understand that all statements about the truth of things necessarily can at most be only partial descriptions of the reality they are trying to describe. This

12

is said to be the case because although reality can be seen from an almost limitless number of perspectives, human language can express things from only one, or perhaps a very few, perspectives at once. This is now also seen to be true of our so-called scientific truths. A fortiori it is the case concerning statements about the truths of the meaning of things. The very fact of dealing with the truth of the "meaning" of something indicates that the knower is essentially involved and hence reflects the perspectival character of all such statements. A statement may be true, of course, i.e., it may accurately describe the extramental reality it refers to, but it will always be cast in particular categories, language, concerns, etc., of a particular "standpoint," and in that sense always will be limited, deabsolutized. This also is a perspectival view of truth, and therefore also relational.

Moreover, the limited and limiting, as well as liberating, quality of language is especially seen when there is talk of the transcendent. By definition the transcendent is that which goes beyond our experience. Hence, all statements about the transcendent are seen to be extremely deabsolutized and limited even beyond the limiting factor of the perspectival character of statements.

4. Hermeneutics: Hans-Georg Gadamer and Paul Ricoeur recently led the way in the development of the science of hermeneutics, which argues that all knowledge of a text is also an interpretaiton of the text, thereby still further deabsolutizing claims about the "true" meaning of the text. But this basic insight goes beyong the knowledge of a text and applies to all knowledge. Some of the key notions here can be compressed in the following mantra (a mantra is a seven-syllable phrase which capsulizes an insight): "Subject, object, two is one." The whole of hermeneutics is here in nuce: All knowledge is interpreted knowledge; the perceiver is part of the perceived, especially, but not only, in the humane disciplines; the subject is part of the object. When the object of study is some aspect of humanity, it is obvious that the observer is also the observed, which "deobjectivizes," deabsolutizes the resultant knowledge, truth. The same, however, is also fundamentally true, though in a different way, of all knowledge, truth, of the natural sciences, for various aspects of nature are observed only through the categories we provide, within the horizon we establish, under the paradigm we uti-

13

lize, in response to the questions we raise, and in relationship to the connections we make--a further deabsolutizing of truth, even of the "hard" sciences.

To move on to the second half of the mantra, "two is one": We see that knowledge comes from the subject perceiving the object but since the subject is also part of the object, the two therefore are one in that sense. Also, in knowing, the object as such is taken up into the subject, and thus again the two are one. And yet, there is also a radical twoness there, for it is the very process of the two becoming one (or, alternatively, the two being perceived as one, or even better, the becoming aware that the two, which are very really two, are also in fact very really one) that is what we call knowing. This is an interpretative view of truth. It is clear that relationality pervades this hermeneutical, interpretative, view of truth.

A further development of this basic insight is that I learn by dialogue, i.e., not only by being open to, receptive, in a passive sense, of extramental reality, but by having a dialogue with extramental reality. I not only "hear," receive, reality, but I also--and I think, first of all--"speak" to reality. That is, I ask it questions, I stimulate it to speak back to me, to answer my questions. Furthermore, I give reality the specific categories, language with which, in which, to speak, to respond to me. It can "speak" to me, i.e., really communicate to my mind only in a language, in categories, that I understand. When the speaking, the responding, becomes more and more ununderstandable to me, I slowly begin to become aware that there is a new language being developed here and that I must learn it if I am to make sense out of what reality is saying to me. This is a dialogic view of truth, whose very name reflects its relationality.

With this new, and irreversible, understanding of the meaning of truth, the critical thinker has undergone a radical Copernican turn. Just as the greatly resisted shift in astronomy from geocentrism to heliocentrism revolutionized that science, and much else(!), so too the paradigm or model shift in the understanding of truth statements has revolutionized all the humanities, including theology-ideology. The macro paradigm or macro model with which critical thinkers operate today (or the "horizon" within which they operate, to use Bernard Lonergan's term) is characterized by historical, social, linguistic,

hermeneutical, praxis, relational and dialogic consciousness. This paradigm or model shift is far
advanced among thinkers and doers; but as with
Copernicus, and even more dramatically with Galileo,
there are still many resisters in positions of great
institutional power.

It is difficult to overestimate the importance of
the role played by the conceptual paradigm or model one
has of reality in the understanding of reality and how
to live accordingly. The paradigm or model within
which we perceive reality not only profoundly affects
our intellectual understanding of reality, but it also
has immense practical consequences. For example (as
pointed out by Henry Rosemont, Fulbright Professor of
Philosophy at Fudan University, Shanghai, 1982-84), in
Western medicine the body is usually conceived of under
the model of a highly nuanced, living machine, and,
therefore, if one part wears out, the obvious thing to
do is to replace the worn part--hence, organ trans-
plants originated in Western medicine. However, in
Oriental, Chinese, medicine, the body is conceived of
under the model of a finely balanced harmony: if
"pressure" is exerted on one part of the body, it is
assumed that it has an opposite effect in some other
part of the body--hence, acupuncture originated in
Oriental medicine. Furthermore, obviously some
attempts at perceiving reality through a particular
paradigm or model will fit the data better than others,
and they will then be preferred--e.g., the shift from
the geocentric to the heliocentric model in astronomy.
But sometimes different models will both in their own
ways "fit" the data more or less as well--as in the
example of Western and Oriental medicines. The differing models would then be viewed as complementary.
Clearly it would be foolish to limit one's perception
of reality to only one of the complementary paradigms
or models. Perhaps at times a more comprehensive
model, a mega-model, can be conceived to subsume the
two or more complementary models, but surely it will
never be possible to perceive reality except through
paradigms or models; hence <u>meta</u>-model thinking is not
possible, except in the more limited sense of meta-
<u>monomodel</u> thinking, that is, perceiving reality through
multiple, differing models which cannot be subsumed
under one megamodel, but must stand in creative, polar
tension in relationship to each other. Such might be
called multi-model thinking.[4]

With the deabsolutized view of the truth of the meaning of things we come face to face with the specter of relativism, which is the opposite pole of absolutism. Unlike relationality, which is a neutral term, merely denoting the quality of being in relationship, relativism is a basically negative term (as "isms" often are). If one can no longer claim that any statement of the truth of the meaning of things is absolute, totally objective, because the claim does not square with our experience of reality, it is equally impossible to claim that every statement of the truth of the meaning of things is completely relative, totally subjective, for that also does not square with our experience of reality, and furthermore would logically lead to an atomizing solipsism (self-alone-ism) which would stop all discourse, all statements to others.

Our perception, and hence description, of reality is like viewing an object in the center of a circle of viewers. My view and description of the object (reality) will be true, but it will not include what someone on the other side of the circle perceives and describes, which will also be true. So, neither of the perceptions/descriptions of the object (reality) is total, complete--"absolute" in that sense--or "objective" in the sense of not in any way being dependent on a "subject." At the same time, however, it is also obvious that there is an "objective," doubtless "true" aspect to each perception/description, even though each is relational to the perceiver-"subject."

At the same time that the always partial, perspectival, deabsolutized view of all truth statements is recognized, the common human basis for perceptions-descriptions of reality and values must also be kept in mind. All human beings experience certain things in common. We all experience our bodies, pain, pleasure, hunger, satiation, etc., etc. Our cognitive faculties perceive certain structures in reality, e.g., variation and symmetries in pitch, color, form, etc. All humans experience affection, dislike, etc. Here, and in other commalities, are the bases for building a universal, fundamental epistemology, aesthetics, value systems, etc. Of course it will be vital to distinguish carefully between those human experiences/perceptions which come from nature and those which come from nurture. However, because in some instances nurture can override nature, it will at times be difficult to discern precisely where the distinction is. In fact, all of our "natural" experiences will be more or less shaped by our "nurturing," that is, all of our experience, knowledge, will be interpreted through the lens of our "nurturing" structures.

But if we can no longer hold to an absolutist view of the truth of the meaning of things, we must take certain steps so as not to be logically forced into the silence of total relativism, including at least the following two: One, besides striving to be as accurate and fair as possible in our gathering and assessing of information, submitting it to the critiques of our peers and other thinkers and scholars, we need also to dredge out, state clearly, and analyze our own presuppositions--but this is a constant, ongoing task. However, even in doing this we will be operating from a particular "standpoint." Therefore, we need, secondly, to complement out constantly critiqued statements with statements from different "standpoints." That is, we need to engage in dialogue with those who have differing cultural, philosophical, social, religious viewpoints so as to strive toward an ever fuller--but never completely full--perception of the truth of the meaning of things. If we do not engage in such dialogue we will not only be trapped within the perspective of our own "standpoint," we will now also know it. Hence, we will no longer with integrity deliberately be able to remain turned in on ourselves. Our search for the truth of the meaning of things makes it a necessity for us as human beings that we engage in dialogue. Knowingly to refuse dialogue today could be an act of fundamental human irresponsibility--in Judeo-Christian terms, a sin.

Paul Knitter noted much the same thing particularly in the shift in the model of truth from the former exclusivistically either-or model to the dialogic or relational model: "In the new model, truth will no longer be identified by its ability to exclude or absorb others. Rather, what is true will reveal itself mainly by its ability to relate to other expressions of truth and to grow through these relationships: truth defined not by exclusion but by relation. The new model reflects what our pluralistic world is discovering: no truth can stand alone; no truth can be totally unchangeable. Truth, by its very nature, needs other truth. If it cannot relate, its quality of truth must be open to question."[5]

If this is true for all human beings in the search for the truth of the meaning of things, it is most

17

intensely so for religious persons and those committed to ideologies, such as Marxism. Religions and ideologies describe and prescribe for the whole of life; they are holistic, all-encompassing, and therefore tend to blot out, that is, either convert or condemn, outsiders even more than other institutions which are not holistic. Thus the need for due modesty in truth claims and complementarity for particular views of the truth, as described above, is most intense in the field of religion.

But the need for dialogue in religion and ideology is also intensified in the modern world because slowly through the impact of mass communications and the high level of mobility of contemporary society in the West, and elsewhere, we more and more experience "others" as living holistic, "holy" lives--not in spite of, but because of their religion or ideology. To be concrete: when I as a Christian come to know Jews as religious persons who are leading whole, holy, human lives out of the fullness of their Judaism, I am immediately confronted with the question: What is the source of this holiness, this wholeness? It obviously is not Christianity. Unless I really work at duping myself, I cannot say that it is unconscious or anonymous Christianity, for if there is any religion which has for two thousand years consciously rejected Christianity, that religion is Judaism. Clearly, the only possible answer is that the source of the holiness, the wholeness, of the Jew is the Jewish religion, and the God who stands behind it, the God of Abraham, Isaac, Jacob--and Yeshua. Using traditional theological language "from above," it should be noted that Christianity, like Judaism, is a religion that believes that God reveals her/himself to us through events and persons; to learn God's message, God's Torah, good news, Gospel, we Christians must seek to listen to God wherever and through whomever he/she speaks, that is, we must be in dialogue with persons of other religions to learn what God is saying to us through them.

III. GROUND RULES FOR INTERRELIGIOUS, INTERIDEOLOGICAL DIALOGUE

We are here then speaking of a specific kind of dialogue, an interreligious, interideological dialogue. To have such, it is not sufficient that the dialogue partners discuss a religious-ideological subject, that is, the meaning of life and how to live accordingly. Rather, they must come to the dialogue as persons somehow significantly identified with a religious or ideological community. If I were neither a Christian nor a Marxist, for example, I could not participate as a "partner" in a Christian-Marxist dialogue, though I might listen in, ask some questions for information, and make some helpful comments.

The following are some basic ground rules of interreligious, interideological dialogue that must be observed if dialogue is actually to take place. These are not theoretical rules given from "on high," but ones that have been learned from hard experience.

First Rule: <u>The primary purpose of dialogue is to learn, that is, to change and grow in the perception and understanding of reality and then to act accordingly.</u> We come to dialogue that <u>we</u> might learn, change, and grow, not that we might force change on the <u>other</u>, as one hopes to do in debate--a hope which is realized in inverse proportion to the frequency and ferocity with which debate is entered into. On the other hand, because in dialogue <u>each</u> partner comes with the intention of learning and changing him or herself, one's partner in fact will also change. Thus the alleged goal of debate, and much more, is accomplished far more effectively by dialogue.

Second Rule: <u>Interreligious, interideological dialogue must be a two-sided project--within each religious or ideological community and between religious or ideological communities.</u> Because of the "corporate" nature of interreligious, interideological dialogue, and since the primary goal of dialogue is that each partner learn and change herself, it is also necessary that each participant enter into dialogue not only with her partner across the faith line--the Catholic with the Protestant, for example--but also with her coreligionists, with her fellow Catholics, to share with them the fruits of the interreligious dialogue. Only thus can the whole community eventually learn and change, moving toward an ever more perceptive insight into reality.

Third Rule: <u>Each participant must come to the dialogue with complete honesty and sincerity.</u> It should be made clear in what direction the major and minor thrusts of the tradition move, what the future shifts might be, and, if necessary, where the participant has difficulties with his/her own tradition. No false fronts have any place in dialogue.

Conversely--each participant must assume a similar complete honesty and sincerity in the other partners. Not only will the absence of sincerity prevent dialogue from happening, the absence of the assumption of the partners' sincerity will do so as well. In brief: no trust, no dialogue.

Fourth Rule: In interreligious, interideological dialogue we must not compare our ideals with our partner's practice, but rather our ideals with our partner's ideals, our practice with our partner's practice.

Fifth Rule: Each participant must define herself. Only the Jew, for example, can define from the inside what it means to be a Jew. The rest can only describe what it looks like from the outside. Moreover, because dialogue is a dynamic medium, as each participant learns, she will change and hence continually deepen, expand, and modify her self-definition as a Jew--being careful to remain in constant dialogue with her fellow Jews. Thus it is mandatory that each dialogue partner herself define what it means to be an authentic member of her own tradition.

Conversely--the one interpreted must be able to recognize herself in the interpretation. This is the golden rule of interreligious, interideological hermeneutics, as has been often reiterated by the "apostle of interreligious dialogue," Raimundo Panikkar.[6] For the sake of understanding, each dialogue participant will naturally attempt to express for herself what she thinks is the meaning of the partner's statement; the partner must be able to recognize herself in that expression. The advocate of "a world theology," Wilfred Cantwell Smith, would add that the expression must also be verifiable by critical observers not involved.[7]

Sixth Rule: Each participant must come to the dialogue with no hard-and-fast assumptions as to where the points of disagreement are. Rather, each partner should not only listen to the other partner with openness and sympathy, but also attempt to agree with the dialogue partner as far as is possible while still maintaining integrity with his own tradition; where he absolutely can agree no further without violating his own integrity, precisely there is the real point of disagreement--which most often turns out to be different from the point of disagreement that was falsely assumed ahead of time.

Seventh Rule: <u>Dialogue</u> <u>can</u> <u>take</u> <u>place</u> <u>only</u>
<u>between</u> <u>equals</u>, as Vatican II put it: <u>Par</u> <u>cum</u> <u>pari</u>.
Both must come to learn from each other. Therefore,
if, for example, the Muslim views Hinduism as inferior,
or if the Hindu views Islam as inferior, there will be
no dialogue. If authentic interreligious, interideological dialogue between Muslims and Hindus is to occur,
then both the Muslim and the Hindu must come mainly to
learn from each other; only then will it be "equal with
equal," <u>par</u> <u>cum</u> <u>pari</u>.

Eighth Rule: <u>Dialogue</u> <u>can</u> <u>take</u> <u>place</u> <u>only</u> <u>on</u> <u>the</u>
<u>basis</u> <u>of</u> <u>mutual</u> <u>trust</u>. Although interreligious, inter-
ideological dialogue must occur with some kind of
"corporate" dimension, that is, the participants must
be involved as members of a religious or ideological
community--for instance, as Marxists or Taoists--it is
also fundamentally true that it is only <u>persons</u> who can
enter into dialogue. But a dialogue among persons can
be built only on personal trust. Hence it is wise not
to tackle the most difficult problems in the beginning,
but rather to approach first those issues most likely
to provide some common ground, thereby establishing the
basis of human trust. Then, gradually, as this personal trust deepens and expands, the more thorny matters can be undertaken. Thus, as in learning we move
from the known to the unknown, so in dialogue we
proceed from commonly held matters--which, given our
mutual ignorance resulting from centuries of hostility,
will take us quite some time to discover fully--to
discuss matters of disagreement.

Ninth Rule: <u>A</u> <u>person</u> <u>entering</u> <u>into</u> <u>interreli-</u>
<u>gious</u>, <u>interideological</u> <u>dialogue</u> <u>must</u> <u>be</u> <u>at</u> <u>least</u> <u>mini-</u>
<u>mally</u> <u>self-critical</u> <u>of</u> <u>both</u> <u>oneself</u> <u>and</u> <u>one's</u> <u>own</u>
<u>religious</u> <u>or</u> <u>ideological</u> <u>tradition</u>. A lack of such
self-criticism implies that one's own tradition already
has all the correct answers. Such an attitude not only
makes dialogue unnecessary, but even impossible, since
we enter into dialogue primarily so <u>we</u> can learn--which
obviously is impossible if our tradition has never made
a misstep, if it has all the right answers. To be
sure, in interreligious, interideological dialogue one
must stand within a religious or ideological tradition
with integrity and conviction, but such integrity and
conviction must include, not exclude, a healthy self-
criticism. Without it there can be no dialogue--and,
indeed, no integrity.

21

Tenth Rule: Each participant eventually must attempt to experience the partner's religion or ideology "from within"; for a religion or ideology is not merely something of the head, but also of the spirit, heart and "whole being," individual and communal. John Dunne here speaks of "passing over" into another's religious or ideological experience and then coming back enlightened, broadened and deepened.

IV. DIALOGUE AREAS

Interreligious, interideological dialogue operates in three areas: the practical, where we collaborate to help humanity; the depth or "spiritual" dimension, where we attempt to experience the partner's religion or ideology "from within"; the cognitive, where we seek understanding and truth. Interreligious, interideological dialogue also has three phases. In the first phase (which we never completely outgrow) we unlearn misinformation about each other and begin to know each other as we truly are. In phase two we begin to discern values in the partner's tradition and wish to appropriate them into our own tradition. For example, in the Buddhist-Christian dialogue, Christians might learn a greater appreciation of the meditative tradition, and Buddhists might learn a greater appreciation of the prophetic, social justice tradition--both values traditionally strongly, though not exclusively, associated with the other's community. If we are serious, persistent and sensitive enough in the dialogue, we may at times enter into phase three. Here we together begin to explore new areas of reality, of meaning, of truth, of which neither of us had even been aware before. We are brought face to face with this new, as yet unknown to us dimension of reality only because of questions, insights, probings produced in the dialogue. We may thus dare to say that patiently pursued dialogue can become an instrument of new "re-velation," a further "un-veiling" of reality--on which we must then act.

1. Dialogue In Practice

Religions and ideologies are not only explanations of the meaning of life, but also ways (e.g., Hodos, Christianity; Halacha, Judaism; Shar'ia, Islam; Tao, Chinese religion) to live according to that explanation. For example, the Buddhist is not only to seek liberation interiorly, but also to practive the virtues of justice, honesty, compassion, etc. In Judaism the

22

prophetic tradition of social justice is even encoded into specific laws in the Talmud. At the beginnings of Christianity Jesus said that those are saved who feed the hungry, clothe the naked, house the homeless, instruct the ignorant, etc.; St. John said that whoever says he loves God but hates his brother is a liar; St. James said that faith without works is dead. Marxism also offers not just a social theory, but also a social program and practice.

Many human problems are of a pressing nature that call forth social action on the part of many different religions and ideologies: peace, hunger, discrimination, social justice, human rights, etc. In many instances joint action on these concrete problems will be more effective than several individual, parallel or even duplicative actions. This actual cooperation for the good of humanity will also break down barriers between the religions and ideologies and will lead to conscious dialogue about the respective self-understandings and motivations that underlie the commitment to the action by the different religions and ideologies involved. For example, the Christians and the atheistic humanists who ended up in the Selma, Alabama, jail together because of their marching with Martin Luther King for equal rights for Blacks in America entered into dialogue to learn how their differing faiths and ideologies led to the same radical action.

Interreligious, interideological action that does not eventually lead to dialogue will end by becoming mindless, and hence ineffective. Interreligious, interideological dialogue that does not eventually lead to action will end by being hypocritical, and hence, ineffective.

2. Depth or "Spiritual" Dialogue

In the area of depth or "spiritual" dialogue we experience the partner's religion or ideology "from within." Raimundo Panikkar speaks of this when he says, "religious dialogue must be genuinely religious, not merely an exchange of doctrines or intellectual opinions. . . . dialogue must proceed from the depths of my religious attitude to these same depths in my partner."[8] He even goes so far as to state: "I 'left' as a Christian; I 'found' myself a Hindu; and I 'returned' as a Buddhist, without having ceased to be a Christian."[9] Perhaps such double or multiple "belonging" is not possible for most religious persons, for most religious thinkers, or those ideologically committed, but experiencing another's religion or ideology "from within" at least to some extent is possible for all. John Dunne's "passing over" is one very effective means for doing so. He describes it thus: "Passing over is a shifting of standpoint, a going over to the standpoint of another culture, another way of life, another religion. It is followed by an equal and opposite process we might call 'coming back,' coming back with new insight to one's own culture, one's own way of life, one's own religion."[10]

Here imagination plays a key role. After entering into the feelings of one's partner and permitting her symbols, stories, etc. to stimulate images in one's own mind, these images are to be allowed to move, leading one where they will, so that eventually one will return to one's own tradition--greatly enriched. Dunne describes it thus: "the technique of passing over is based on the process of eliciting images from one's feelings, attaining insights into the images, and then turning insight into a guide of life. What one does in passing over is to try to enter sympathetically into the feelings of another person, become receptive to the images which give expression to his feelings, attain insight into those images, and then come back enriched by this insight to an understanding of one's own life which can guide one into the future."[11]

Moreover, as Paul Knitter notes, "passing over, while it is mainly the work of the imagination, also requires some hard intellectual homework. . . . and proves that although one never attains a final answer, one can come to more answers, real answers. The imagination is persistently excited; new insights are born; the horizon of knowledge expands. Interreligious dialogue, like all life, is seen not as a nervous pursuit of certainty but a freeing, exciting pursuit of understanding."[12] Knitter also points out that David Tracy's The Analogical Imagination "might be read as a handbook of guidelines on the nature of dialogue with other traditions and the pivotal role of the imagination in such dialogue."[13] Tracy confirms "the possibilities of approaching the conversation among the religious traditions through the use of an analogical imagination. . . . If I have already lived by an analogical imagination within my own religious and cultural heritage, I am much more likely to welcome the demand for futher conversation."[14]

3. A Universal Systematic Reflection (Theology) of Religion-Ideology

But what of the cognitive area (which of course must not be isolated from the practical and depth or "spiritual" areas), where perhaps the greatest challenge to interreligious, interideological dialogue lies? How can one proceed beyond mutually informative lectures? I believe the question can be helpfully phrased as follows: In reflecting upon my own religious or ideological belief, that is, in Christian terminology, in "theologizing," how can I speak so that I on the one hand maintain integrity with my own religious, ideological convictions and tradition, and on the other allow my dialogue partner to understand and recognize her or himself in my language? To be concrete, how can I as a Christian speak about the central insights of my faith in such a way that the Jew, or the Marxist, or indeed both, would be able to say, "Yes, that sounds like familiar territory. I feel somehow included in those concepts, terms, images, etc., although I might not traditionally use precisely the same ones in my own faith or ideological reflections, that is, 'theologizing'"?

To put the problem in a positive way, we who are convinced of not only the advantage but also the necessity of interreligious, interideological dialogue (for not only the bene esse, but even the esse of creative religious, ideological reflection today), need to work together to forge a "universal systematic reflection (theology) of religion-ideology." I am aware that there are difficulties already in this naming of the project. However, any naming of a project with such a comprehensive scope will necessarily have difficulties entailed. There is no way that we can speak of things except within a particular cultural framework, no matter how broad the cultural framework might be. Even an extremely broad cultural framework is particular and would automatically be other than a whole range of other particular cultural frameworks, and one would then have to justify the choice of that cultural framework rather than another. In fact, the choice of this particular cultural framework is not essential. What is essential is simply the choice of a particular cultural framework. I have chosen the one that I personally am most familiar with so that I might explain most clearly precisely what is meant, and thereby, I hope, eliminate possible confusions through unclarity.

By theology here is simply meant a systematic, reasoned reflection upon the convictions, the "religious," or "ideological" convictions that are held by one or more human beings. (The term "philosophy" would seem inadequate here, for it often means a reasoned reflection which does not include sources of wisdom in a tradition outside of ratiocination. Though "theology" is largely a Christian term--the pre-Christian Greeks invented it, however--it has the advantage of including both reasoning and other wisdom sources in a tradition, e.g., "sacred" books--whether the Bible, the Qur'an, the Vedas, or Das Kapital. Hence despite its theistic and Christian particularity, until a better term is found, or forged, I shall utilize the shorthand "theology" to refer to the systematic reasoned reflections upon the "religious" or "ideological" convictions held by human communities.) In speaking of a universal theology of religion-ideology, I mean to indicate all the insights of a faith or ideology which attempts to explain the meaning of life and how to live accordingly--whether that includes the notion of "Theos" or not. What makes it universal is that the categories of reflection are such that they can be understood and embraced by persons of all religions or ideologies, not just a particular one, or particular set, e.g., Christianity, the Abrahamic religions, the theistic religions.

If that is the task, the way forward, I believe, is for the thinkers in each religious and ideological tradition to attempt to express their reflections, their "theologizing," in categories, terms, images, that the "others" will not only be able to understand, but also in which they will feel included, as was stated above. But this seems, in fact, like an impossible task. How can Christians, for example, speak of the insights into the meaning of human life given them by the Christian tradition in categories, terms, images other than Christian ones? In fact, it seems to me that Christians do already something of that sort, at least in some instances. Christians very often speak a language which is extremely familiar to Jews. When it is recollected that Yeshua was not a Christian but a Jew, and all his first followers were Jews, and that perhaps the majority of our prayers, etc. come from the Hebrew Bible, such a fact is no longer a surprise. The additional fact that Mohammed also looked upon the Hebrew Bible and the New Testament as sacred books also means that much of our Christian language will likewise be familiar to Muslims. So,

Christians might try to do some of their reflecting using only a vocabulary that would in fact be familiar to the other two Abrahamic religions. Indeed, this is precisely the sort of thing that can reasonably be attempted within the framework of a Trialogue.

However, modern critical thinkers immediately have a difficulty even in this relatively limited step toward "a universal theology of religion-ideology." Much of the language of the Jewish and Christian traditions no longer finds a clear resonance among many Jews and Christians who have been bred in the atmosphere of modern critical thought. (Of course this does not mean that modern critical thinkers are automatically somehow less religious or committed than "pre-critical" thinkers. Indeed, a moment's recollection will recall that Moses, Jesus, and Mohammed were extremely "critical" thinkers in the religious sphere vis-à-vis what existed up until their time. In fact, it was the very radicalness of their "critical" thinking that made them the fountain-heads of new religious streams.) For such critical thinkers language needs to be found which will effectively communicate the authentic insights of the religious tradition in ways that will find true resonance in understanding and life.

V. "ECUMENICAL ESPERANTO"

It is precisely this challenge from within the Jewish and Christian traditions, this demand for a language, a way of understanding the ancient religious insights in terms of critical thought, that, I believe, points to us the way to go forward in trying to forge a "universal theology of religion-ideology." We must build our "theological" language, terms, categories, images, etc., on our common humanity. It is that which the traditional Jew, Christian, Muslim, the modern critical thinker, Hindu, Buddhist, Marxist, etc. share in common. To the extent that we can speak of a religious, ideological insight in such "humanity-based" language, to that extent we will be building a "universal theology of religion-ideology." Put in other words, we must attempt to cast our religious and ideological insights in language "from below," that is, from our humanity, and not "from above," not from the perspective of the transcendent, the divine. From a slightly different perspective, we must attempt to develop a "theological" language which is "from within," not "from without." We must try to speak a language of immanence, not of transcendence. This does

27

not mean that religious persons should no longer speak of, let alone believe in, the transcedent. No, I mean that in this particular task of forging a "universal theology of religion-ideology" we must learn to speak of the transcendent in immanent terms, imagery, categories, etc. This new "theological" language "from below," "from within," which is immanent rather than transcendent, might be helpfully called a theological-ideological "Esperanto," for, like Esperanto is supposed to be, it is an intercultural language that takes something from various living languages, but is so simplified, so "rational," so "generally human," that anyone with the knowledge of his own native tongue and a bit more of other tongues will easily be able to master it. Moreover, the point of Esperanto is to facilitate communication on a broad international, intercultural level. Esperanto was never intended to take the place of all or even of any of the world's living languages. Rather, it was merely to be an international supplementary language, but as such it would be of immense value.

Now here, I believe, the analogy breaks down, or at least I hope it will, for in fact Esperanto has not been a success in terms of its goal. Perhaps only twenty million people throughout the whole of the world know Esperanto; hence it can hardly fulfill its stated function. (Further, it is based only on an Indo-European language culture.) The "ecumenical (universal) Esperanto" of the "universal theology of religion-ideology" of which I am speaking must go beyond gaining the adherence of a relatively small coterie of theological-ideological thinkers in various religious-ideological traditions. If it does not do so, it will in fact suffer the fate, to a large extent at least, that Esperanto has in the linguistic world. We ought, therefore not be like the fool who learns from his own mistakes, but rather like the wise man who learns from the mistakes of others, and effectively work to make "ecumenical Esperanto" a vitalizing means of developing a "universal theology of religion-ideology."

We probably can find a little more help in the analogy of learning a foreign language when speaking about developing a "universal theology of religion-ideology." One of the fundamental things that must be done in learning a new language is to learn to "hear," to "discern" the new sounds, or those sounds which at least to us seem new. This is usually the more difficult the older the person is--that is, the more that we are used to and steeped in our own particular linguistic sounds, or, to speak of our primary subject here, used to and steeped in our own particular religious, theological, ideological, language--categories, terms, images, stories, etc. Moreover, all of our religious traditions have grown up and developed in an era when the tendency was to speak "from above," "from without," from the perspective of the transcendent, of God. Hence it is going to be especially difficult for us to "attune" our theological, our religious ears to hearing the same "meaning" in those different sounds of that other language which is so strange to our traditions, namely, that "ecumenical Esperanto," "from below," "from within," of immanence rather than transcendence, or perhaps better said, transcendence within immanence. Ideologies, like Marxism, for example, on the other hand, may have greater difficulty discovering the depth or "spiritual" dimension. We all in fact have before us not only the gigantic task of developing a new language, an "ecumenical Esperanto," but also at the same time the even more challenging taks of forging a "new consciousness" which will be capable of "hearing" and "understanding" this new "ecumenical Esperanto." Clearly this task is not one that can be performed in two sequential steps, one after the other. Rather, it must be carried out in dialectical, dialogical fashion, with a constant back and forth, interplay, mutuality between the forming of the new language, the "ecumenical Esperanto," and the new consciousness, the "ecumenical consciousness." However, what could be more fitting as a method of carrying out the task of providing a "theology" for worldwide interreligious, interideological dialogue?[15]

Because interreligious, interideological dialogue is always necessarily a two-sided project--within each religious or ideological community as well as between religious and ideological communities--at least one further step in this process is necessary. I have noted above that it is also necessary that each interreligious, interideological dialogue participant enter into dialogue not only with her partner across the faith-ideology line, but also with her coreligionists, coideologists, to share with them the fruits of the interreligious, interideological dialogue, since only thus can the whole community eventually learn, change, and grow toward an even more perceptive insight into reality. In order to fulfill this intra-religious, intraideological dialogue as the other half

of the interreligious, interideological dialogue, which
is making use of the "ecumenical Esperanto" and forging
a new "ecumenical consciousness" to hear and understand
that new "universal theology of religion-ideology," it
is necessary all along the way to make the connections
between the newly formed "ecumenical Esperanto" and
each of the traditional religious languages: When we
say "X" in "ecumenical Esperanto," that corresponds to
"A" in Christianity, "B" in Judaism, "C" in Marxism,
etc.   Thus we will really be able to talk to and
understand each other to a large extent by means of the
"translation" of our traditional languages into the
"ecumenical Esperanto."   However, we must at the same
time note that, just as in all translations in the
linguistic area, no translation is precisely the same
as the original.   Therefore, although "X" will be
perhaps essentially, fundamentally, the same as "A,"
"B," "C," etc., none of them will be precisely the same
as each other.   This, of course, is not something to be
deplored, but on the contrary, something to be deeply
appreciated.   All life is very complicated, and human
life is the most complicated.   For anyone to be able to
express and understand all of the complexities of human
life, that person would have to be as comprehensive as
all the human persons who have ever lived, who ever
will live, and who ever could live.   When one adds to
this the further, indeed, infinite complexity (if one
can thus speak) of the transcendent related to all
humanity, actual and possible, it is clear that one
would have to be fully divine in order to utter such an
all-comprehending notion--and similarly divine to
understand it.   Obviously this we cannot do--hence, the
absolute necessity of our attempting to gain an ever
fuller insight into the meaning of human life by a
dialogue with an ever fuller set of expressions of that
meaning.   In other words: Variety, yes, even to
infinity; but with an access to that variety by way of
an adequate simplicity which will facilitate and not
obfuscate understanding.

It must also be borne in mind that when speaking
of "ecumenical Esperanto" I am not recommending some
sort of pale, reductionist, least common denominator
kind of "theological" expression.   I am not speaking of
a "theology" that will be more superficial than our
present particular ones, but rather one that is more
profound, that goes even more deeply into our psyches,
individual and communal.   "Ecumenical Esperanto" must
not be simply a superficial Enlightenment rationality
warmed up again.   No, it must go far beyond that and

also include all the advances made in our understanding of knowledge referred to earlier, in history, sociology of knowledge, limitations of language, hermeneutics, plus ideology critique, praxis dialectics, paradigm shift, etc., etc. All these new insights from Western culture must be utilized, but by these very principles it must be seen that they too are necessarily culture-bound. Hence, to be truly "humanity" based, the religious, ideological thinker must also strive to incorporate all insights into what it means to be human, including those insights from outside Western culture. The "we" implicit in the terms "from below" and "from within" must be as broad a "we" as possible, in fact an _ever increasingly_ broad "we." And this can be done only by moving beyond--without abandoning--Western culture, beyond Judaism, Christianity, Western humanism, and Marxism, to absorb the insights of Islam, Hinduism, Buddhism, etc. This can be done only by hard study of, "passing over" into the inner heart of, patient and profound dialogue with, other religions, ideologies and cultures.

If I may be permitted a practical note at this point--if anything like this is to be realized, all educated religious and ideologically committed persons, besides studying their own tradition deeply, must also take courses in other religious and ideological traditions, and as much as possible, from persons who not only are trained in but also stand in those religious or ideological traditions so they might have an enhanced chance of learning to know that tradition "from within." If one expands the term ecumenism to include dialogue with all religions and ideologies one finds strong support for this recommendation in both the documents of Vatican II and subsequent Vatican documents: "We _must_ become familiar with the outlook of our separated brethren. Study is _absolutely_ required for this, and it should be pursued in fidelity to the truth and with a spirit of good will. Catholics . . . need to acquire a more adequate understanding of the respective doctrines of our separated brethren, their history, their spiritual and liturgical life, their religious psychology and cultural background. Most valuable for this purpose are meetings of the two sides--especially for discussion of theological problems--where each can treat with the other on an equal footing (_par cum pari_)."[16] The "Directory Concerning Ecumenical Matters," issued by the Secretariat for Christian Unity of the Vatican in 1970, made the point more concrete: "All Christians should be of an ecumenical mind . . . hence, the principles of ecumenism sanctioned by the Second Vatican Council should be appropriately introduced in all institutions of advanced learning. . . . Bishops . . . religious superiors and those in authority in seminaries, universities and similar institutions should take pains to promote the ecumenical movement and spare no effort to see that their teachers keep in touch with advances in ecumenical thought and action."[17] Surely these reflections are valid for all religious and ideological communities.

In the area of Christian missiology a similar point is made by Paul Knitter: "In order to promote the Kingdom, Christians must witness to Christ. All peoples, all religions, must know of him in order to grasp the full content of God's presence in history. Here is part of the purpose and the motivation for going forth to the ends of the earth. But in the new ecclesiology and in the new model for truth, one admits also that all peoples should know of Buddha, of Muhammed, of Krishna [one might also add Socrates, Marx, etc.] This, too, is part of the goal and inspiration for missionary work: to be witnessed to, in order that Christians might deepen and expand their own grasp of God's presence and purpose in the world. Through this mutual witnessing, this mutual growth, the work of realizing the Kingdom moves on."[18]

VI. GOALS OF INTERRELIGIOUS, INTERIDEOLOGICAL DIALOGUE

A number of things have already been said about the goals of interreligious, interideological dialogue, i.e., they are to learn so as to grow, to know the other, to discern and appropriate values, to encounter new dimensions of reality, to witness and be witnessed to, etc. Nevertheless, it would be helpful at this point to try to summarize systematically what the goals of interreligious, interideological dialogue are, and are not.

First, a distinction must be made between intra-Christian (and perhaps intra-Jewish, intra-Muslim, etc.?) dialogue on the one hand, and Christian-Buddhist, Hindu-Muslim, etc. dialogues on the other. The goal of the former is some kind of overarching, "organic," yet pluralistic, unity (not uniformity). A simple, overarching, organic, world religion-ideology is not the goal of interreligious, interideological dialogue. Rather, the goals could be said to be three:

1) to know oneself ever more profoundly; 2) to know the other ever more authentically; 3) to live ever more fully accordingly.

We come to know ourselves largely by contrast, by encountering the other. Concretely: I discovered dimensions of my American cultural heritage only as a result of living for several years in Europe--and my common Western cultural heritage by living in the Orient. Through interreligious, interideological dialogue we will come to know consciously our own religious, ideological selves with all of their consistencies and contradictions, their admirable and abhorrent aspects. Our dialogue partners will serve as mirrors for us, showing us our true selves. Such a prize alone is worth the price of frustration in dialogue.

We do not come to know our partners in dialogue simply as objects over against ourselves. Rather, we learn to know our partners in dialogic fashion, that is, in relationship to us. (Since we are here talking about interreligious, interideological dialogue, we must also keep its corporate nature in mind.) Hence, we come to know what we have in common ever more fully--which, as we know already from experience, will be almost immeasurably more than, and deeper than, we had previously even imagined was possible. But at the same time we will learn to know our true differences (obviously we are not all essentially the same; if we were, there would be no dialogue, only monologue--the death of all human intercourse). These authentic differences will be of two kinds: 1) contradictory, 2) complementary--and we also know from experience already that the latter will most often far outnumber the former.

As indicated before, we must be extremely cautious about "placing" our differences, lest in acting precipitously we mis-place them. So, too, we must not too easily and quickly place our true differences in the contradictory category. For example, it might be that the Hindu moksha, the Zen Buddhist sartori, the Christian "freedom of the children of God," and the Marxist "communist state" could be understood as different, but complementary, descriptions of true human liberation. Further, since we here are speaking of true, though complementary, differences, we are not talking about discerning values in our partner's tradition which we will then wish to appropriate for our own tradition, which was said to occur in phase two of

33

interreligious, interideological dialogue. That indeed does, and should happen, but then we are speaking of something which the two traditions ultimately hold in common, either actually or potentially. But, again, here we are speaking of authentic differences. However, if they are perceived as complementary rather than contradictory, they will be seen to operate within the total organic structure of the other religion-ideology and to fulfill their function properly only within it. It could not have the same function, i.e., relationship to the other parts, in our total organic structure, and hence would not be understood to be in direct opposition, in contradiction to the "differing" elements within our structure.

Nevertheless, we can at times find contradictory truth claims, value claims, between different religious-ideological traditions. That happens only when they cannot be seen as somehow ultimately different expressions of the same thing (a commonality) or as complementary. But when it happens, even though it be relatively rare, a profound, unavoidable problem faces the two communities, namely, what should be their attitude and behavior toward each other? Should they remain in dialogue, tolerate each other, ignore each other, or oppose each other? The problem is especially pressing in matters of value judgments. For example, what does the Christian (or Jew, Muslim, Marxist, or other) do in face of the (fortunately now suppressed) Hindu tradition of widow burning (suttee)? Try to learn its value, tolerate it, ignore it, oppose it (in what manner?)? Or the Nazi ideology's tenet of killing all Jews? These are relatively clear issues, but what of a religion-ideology that approves slavery (as Christianity, Judaism, Islam, etc. did until a century ago)? Perhaps that is clear enough today, but what of sexism--or only a little sexism? Capitalism-socialism? The decision about the proper action becomes less and less clear-cut. It was eventually clear to most non-Hindus in the nineteenth century that the proper attitude toward Hinduism on suttee was not dialogue, but opposition; but apparently it was not so clear to all non-Nazis that oppposition to Jewish genocide was the right stance to take. Further, it took Christians 1800 years to come to that conclusion concerning slavery--but they did come to it. Many religions and ideologies today stand in the midst of a battle over sexism, many of them even refusing to admit that there is such an issue. Finally, no argument need be made

34

concerning the contemporary controversial nature of the capitalism-socialism issue.

Thus, it is apparent that there are important contradictory differences between religions-ideologies, and at times these differences warrant not dialogue, but even opposition. We in fact also make such judgments of "better or worse," of acceptable or not, within religious-ideological traditions--and even do so rather frequently within our individual lives. But surely this exercise of our critical faculties is not to be limited to ourselves and our tradition; this perhaps most human of faculties should be made available to all--with all the proper constraints and concerns for dialogue detailed at length above. We must then ask, on what grounds can we judge whether a religious-ideological difference is in fact contradictory and of such importance and nature as to warrant active opposition? Since all religions and ideologies are attempts to explain the meaning of human life and how to live accordingly, it would seem that those doctrines, customs, etc. which are hostile to human life are to be perceived not as complementary but as contradictory, and that opposition should be proportional to their life-threatening quality. What all is included in an authentically full human life will then have to be the measure against which all elements of all religions-ideologies will have to be tested in making judgments about their being in harmony, complementarity, or contradiction, and then acted upon accordingly. Through dialogue humanity is painfully slowly creeping toward a consensus on what is involved in an authentically full human life. The United Nations Declaration of Human Rights, for example, was a step in that direction. But, of course, more, much, much more consensus needs to be attained if interreligious, interideological dialogue is to reach its full potential.

VII. CONCLUSION

At the same time, however, it is only by means of dialogue that an ever fuller consensus on "the meaning of life and how to live accordingly" will be arrived at. Hence, no systematic reflection--"theology"--can appropriately be done today outside of the matrix of interreligious, interideological dialogue.

[1] *Mirari vos*, 1832, quoted in Leonard Swidler, *Freedom in the Church* (Dayton: Pflaum, 1969), p. 47.

[2] *Ecclesiam suam*, no. 9; emphasis added.

[3] Secretariat for Unbelievers, *Humanae personae dignitatem*, quoted in full in Austin Flannery, *Vatican Council II* (Collegeville, MN: Liturgical Press, 1975), pp. 1003, 1007.

[4] For a full analysis of the notion of the paradigm shift as it applies to theology see Hans Küng's paper "Paradigm Change in Theology," prepared for the international ecumenical symposium "Ein neues Paradigma von Theologie?" held in Tübingen, May 23-26, 1983.

[5] Paul Knitter, *By No Other Name?* (Maryknoll, NY: Orbis, 1984), p. 219.

[6] Raimundo Panikkar, *The Intrareligious Dialogue* (New York: Paulist Press, 1978), p. 30.

[7] Wilfred Cantwell Smith, *Toward a World Theology* (Philadelphia: Westminster Press, 1981), p. 60.

[8] Panikkar, *Intrareligious Dialogue*, p. 50.

[9] Raimundo Panikkar, "Faith and Belief: A Multireligious Experience," *Anglican Theological Review*, 53 (1971), p. 220.

[10] John S. Dunne, *The Way of All the Earth* (New York: Macmillan, 1972), p. ix. Another creative approach might be by way of Ira Progoff's "process mediation."

[11] Ibid., p. 53. For further use of the technique of "passing over" by John Dunne, see his *A Search for God in Time and Memory* (Notre Dame: University of Notre Dame Press, 1977); *The City of the Gods* (Notre Dame: University of Notre Dame Press, 1978).

[12] Knitter, *By No Other Name?*, p. 215.

[13] Ibid.

[14] David Tracy, The Analogical Imagination (New York: Crossroad, 1981), p. 451.

[15] The same notion of the contemporary need of a new consciousness in both intra- and interreligious, interideological dialogue was expressed by Ewert Cousins when speaking of Raimundo Panikkar as a pioneer in its formation: "When Christian consciousness opens to global consciousness, a new type of systematic theology can be born. This new theology calls for a new kind of theologian with a new type of consciousness—a multi-dimensional, cross-cultural consciousness characteristic of mutational man. I believe that Raimundo Panikkar is such a new theologian and that he has already begun to develop such a Christian systematic theology" (Ewert Cousins, "Raimundo Panikkar and the Christian Systematic Theology of the Future," Cross Currents [Summer, 1979], p. 146).

[16] Vatican II, Decree on Ecumenism, no. 9; emphasis added.

[17] Spiritus domini, 1970, nos. 64 and 79. Quoted in full in Flannery, Vatican II, pp. 515, 526.

[18] Knitter, By No Other Name?, p. 222.

GERMANY, CHRISTIANITY AND THE JEWS:
FROM DIATRIBE TO DIALOGUE

by

Leonard Swidler

Germany, the land of Moses Mendelsohn, Heinrich Heine, Reform Judaism, of Karl Marx, Albert Einstein, Hermann Cohen, Franz Rosenzweig and Martin Buber, is also the land of the First Crusade's massacre of Jews, murderous shouts of "Christkillers!", Luther's venemous tirade against "The Jews and Their Lies," of Richard Wagner, National Socialism and Adolf Hitler, the land of the Nuremberg Laws, Kristallnacht, Dachau and Bergen-Belsen. How is it with Jews and Christians in Germany today?

To begin with, there are very few Jews living in Germany today--28,000 in West Germany, largely older Jews, mostly displaced persons from all Europe, and less than 500 in all of East Germany. (Before the war there was a flourishing community of over 500,000 Jews in Germany.)

One must also draw a distinction between East and West Germany. For example, in East Germany there is no public recognition that "we Germans" were responsible for the death of Jews. Rather, it is always "those Facists" who were responsible for killing 300,000 Communists, and also 6,000,000 Jews. There have been relatively few compensatory "reparations" made to Jews. The vast majority of the buildings that were confiscated from the Jews by the Nazis remain Communist government buildings today. Nor is the State of Israel recognized by East Germany.

Quite the opposite of all this is true of West Germany. The West German state and national governments have paid tens of billions of dollars to Jews in "Wiedergutmachung"--reparations. West Germany has been a staunch supporter of the State of Israel. Much of the reparation monies have gone into developing Israel's economy. Although German textbooks, concentration camp museums, television documentaries and forty years of juridicial prosecution of Nazi war criminals have reminded the populace of their own guilty past, the American TV film "Holocaust," seen early in 1979 by almost 20 million West Germans, and the Lansman documentary film Shoah in Spring, 1986, had a massive, profound, and perhaps even long-lasting effect.

But what of Christians and the Christian churches? What is their attitude toward and involvement with Jews and Judaism? Again, a distinction must be made between East and West. There are valiant efforts on the part of a relatively few stalwart Christians in the East, and they must be greatly admired and supported, for they are working against terrific odds and in near-isolation (for details see the two following essays). But in West Germany one can speak of an explosion of sympathy, of concern for, and involvement in Jewish-Christian relations and dialogue since the late 1970's.

The manifestations of this involvement in Jewish-Christian dialogue in Germany can be looked at separately under Catholic, Protestant and Jewish headings, although most often the activities are undertaken cooperatively.

CATHOLIC ACTIVITIES

Catholic Statements

In the past, official statements by the German Catholic Church on the Jews have been neither plentiful nor impressive. There was a Pastoral Letter from the German Bishops in August, 1945, which briefly mentioned that "many Germans, even from among our own ranks, allowed themselves to be fooled by the false teaching of National Socialism, and remained indifferent in the face of crimes against human freedom. Many, through their attitude, encouraged the crimes and many became criminals themselves." In September, 1948, at the huge bi-annual national Catholic Conference, the Katholiken-tag, run by lay and clerical Catholics, a penitential statement was issued which included the following: "In the face of the immense suffering, which like a deluge of crime swept over persons of Jewish extraction and which was unchallenged publicly, the 72nd German Katholikentag confesses in a spirit of Christian penitence toward the past and in a consciousness of responsibility toward the future. . . ."[1]

But there was still no mention by the German hierarchy of the Jews and no indication of the role the

Church played in the catastrophe. The former came in an official document of the German Bishops only in Spring of 1961 when, on the occasion of the trial of Eichmann in Israel, the German Bishops' Conference issued a declaration decrying the crimes committed against the Jewish people and calling upon the German people to make reparations. They also composed a prayer for the murdered Jews and for forgiveness of the guilty ones to be read in all German Catholic churches. There was still no reference to the Church's role in the Holocaust. The same was true of the brief statement by the German bishops in August, 1962, on the eve of the opening of Vatican II: "We call upon our dioceses to make sincere expiation for the terrible crimes which were committed against fundamental human rights by godless authorities in the name of our people."[2]

Then in 1965 at Vatican Council II, the Catholic Church, after almost two thousand years, turned itself around on the issue of its relationship to the Jewish people with the issuance of the Declaration on the Relationship of the Church to Non-Christian Religions. Strangely, however, this revolutionary document had no apparent effect on the official level of the German Catholic Church for some ten years. Then it happened not because of the leadership of the German Bishops, but as a result of the efforts of the lower clergy and laity in November, 1975, at the Joint Synod of the Bishoprics of the Federal Republic of Germany. At last something was said about the role the Church played in the "Final Solution" of the "Jewish Question": "Apart from some admirable efforts by individuals and groups, most of us during the time of National Socialism formed a Church community preoccupied with the threat to our own institutions. We turned our backs to this persecuted Jewish people and were silent about the crimes perpetrated on Jews and Judaism. . . . We deem it the particular duty of the German Church, within the Church as a whole, to work toward a new relationship between Christians and Jews."[3] Though this portion of the Synod document ("Our Hope"), entitled "Toward a New Relationship toward the Jewish People's History of Faith," was a step forward, it disappointingly lagged far behind earlier statements on the official level by the Vatican, the Vienna Archdiocese, Holland, France and the United States.

On November 9, 1978, a further step was taken, this time by the German branch of the Catholic peace organization, Pax Christi. Meeting in conference, Pax

Christi issued a Declaration on the fortieth anniversary of "Reichskristallnacht," the night of nationwide Nazi destruction of synagogues and Jewish property. It stated:

> A specially heavy mortgage weighs on the German people, including the Christians in Germany. They did not stand up decisively and courageously enough against this mass annihilation. And Christianity can not be acquitted on the charge of complicity in the rise of Antisemitism. It was likewise German theologians who over the centuries expounded the notion that the Jews were public enemies. Christians have in the name of God given encouragement to the burning of synagogues and Jewish schools, destroying their houses, obliterating their prayerbooks, banning their faith, hounding them from the streets and confiscating their possessions. [Lutherans will recognize in these words a very close paraphrase of the urgings of Martin Luther in his tirade On the Jews and Their Lies.] Mass forced baptisms, Jew-Masses, and pogroms passed for good works--for they were directed against the "God-killers," as the Jews were denounced by preachers even into our century.[4]

The declaration then went on to recommend the diplomatic recognition of the State of Israel by the Vatican.

Finally, in 1979, two relatively lengthy documents on relations with Jews and Judaism were issued by two separate German Catholic groups, and in 1980 an extensive Declaration on the Relationship of the Church to Judaism by the German Bishops' Conference.

The first document, produced on April 28, 1979, by the Bensberger Circle, a group of progressive Catholics, was prompted by a statement of the Secretariat of the German Bishops' Conference about the television film "Holocaust," which the Bensbergers charged was an act of unacceptable self-justification by the German bishops. The Bensberger Circle insisted on the need for the Catholic Church in Germany to acknowledge openly that "false developments in Church teaching and practice helped to prepare the soil, and jointly created the conditions, through which antisemitism could unfold in such a gruesome manner. . . . It is a decisive fact that the Church did not clearly and unambiguously stand at the side of the Synagogue."[5]

The second group, "Workshop on Jews and Christians" of the Central Committee of Roman Catholics in Germany, a much more broadly based and even quasi-official organization, issued a moderately lengthy and extremely important statement. In a very supportive preface, Bishop Klaus Hemmerle of Aachen, the "Spiritual Assistant" of the Central Committee, stated: "It is such a conversation, without any blurring or circumventing of differences, which is both necessary and possible for the sake of one's own Jewish or Christian existence. It is a discovery in need of translation from the circle of the initiated into the daily routine of the faithful, into the midst of our world. Such a translation has already begun with this document."[6]

The "Workshop on Jews and Christians" has the responsibility of organizing for the Katholikentag (150-year-old biennial Catholic Congress on the order of a Eucharistic Congress). It was at the 1948 Katholikentag that Dr. Karl Thieme, a pioneer in Jewish-Christian dialogue, delivered a lecture about the Jews which led to the positive resolution quoted earlier. And although the concern for Israel and Judaism remained very alive in subsequent Katholikentagen it took time before they established a standing Dialogue Circle of Jews and Christians. This took place in 1970 at the 83rd Katholikentag in Trier. Since then this Circle has engaged in various activities including the establishment of guidelines for Israel tours by German Catholics, collaborating in the investigation of textbooks, and joint planning of conferences at the Catholic Academies and for the Katholikentag.[7] At the 1980 Katholikentag in Berlin, the Orthodox Jewish scholar Professor Pinchas Lapide spoke to an audience of 2,000. Later, Catholics, Protestants and Jews joined in a large memorial and reconciliation march through the streets of Berlin to the Jewish Community Center.

The "Workshop on Jews and Christians," composed of six Jews and seventeen Catholics, worked on their 1979 document, entitled "Basic Theological Issues in Jewish-

43

Christian Dialogue," for three years until they arrived at a unanimous consensus. What gives this document its extraordinary character is the fact that it is truly dialogic. Both the Jews and the Christians came together to learn from each other. Only thus can there be true dialogue. Such mutuality is unfortunately rare in much of what passes for Jewish-Christian dialogue. Two brief quotations will provide a flavor of the outreach attempt of the document:

> The Jewish dialogue partner in conversation with Christians cannot be satisfied with being viewed only as a continuing witness of the so-called Old Testament and of the founding period of the Christian community. On the other hand, the Christian dialogue partner cannot be satisfied if the Jewish dialogue partner believes that only he has something essential for the faith to say to the Christian, whereas that which the Christian has to say to the Jew has no essential significance for Jewish faith. . . .

> Jews can acknowledge that Jesus had become for Christians the Way to find the God of Israel. . . . Christians understand Jesus' fulfillment of the Law and Promises only when they follow him "for the sake of the Reign of Heaven," and thereby attend to his word: "Not everyone who says to me, 'Lord! Lord!' will come into the Reign of Heaven, only the one who fulfills the will of my Father in Heaven" (Mt. 7:21).[8]

On April 28, 1980, the German Bishops' Conference issued a lengthy Declaration (68,000 words) "On the Relationship of the Church to Judaism." It was the fruit of the efforts of a committee of the Conference formed in 1976 under the chairmanship of Bishop Karl Flügel, Auxiliary of the Diocese of Regensburg. The major writer of the document was Professor Franz Mussner, Professor of New Testament at the University of Regensburg. Though the statement does not break any new ground and in some ways still falls short of the earlier Dutch, French, American and Vatican statements (e.g., there is no discussion of the State of Israel or of proselytization), and also far short of what Professor Mussner had written in his _Tractate on the Jews_,[9] it still marks a major step forward. Among other things, the German Bishops stated:

> In Germany we have special reason to ask the pardon of God and our Jewish brethren. Even as we gratefully recall that many Christians, sometimes at great sacrifice to themselves, concerned themselves with Jews, we may not and wish not to forget or suppress the knowledge of what was committed in the midst of our people.[10]

Dr. Ernest Ludwig Ehrlich, a Jewish scholar who has worked closely and sympathetically with the European Christian Churches, had the following critique of the Bishops' Declaration:

> A not inconsiderable minority in the German Bishops' Conference had the intention, and felt the pressing need, to issue a declaration on the Jews which would lead German Catholics and would provide authentic assistance and witness to how German Catholics should reflect on these problems today. Unfortunately this circle of men did not succeed. . . . A great opportunity has been passed up. Not a few outstanding personalities who worked on this text wished, along with us, for a stronger statement, one which did not simply repeat what had already appeared in magisterial Church documents.[11]

A Catholic scholar who was critical of the Declaration also noted, however: "What is said here as an 'official doctrinal declaration' in comparison with what the Church has taught in the past two thousand years about the Jews, is sensationally new. As an official doctrinal declaration this document marks a point from which one may not retreat and it lays the foundation upon which one may--and must--build further."[12]

For several years there have been regular meetings on the international level between the Vatican Committee for Religious Relations with the Jews and the International Jewish Committee on Interreligious Consultations. It was at one of these meetings that the extremely important working paper by Professor Tommaso Federici of Rome was delivered.[13] In the Fall of 1979 the first international Vatican-Jewish meeting was held on German soil at Regensburg, with Bishop Flügel as host, assisted by Professor Mussner.

Religious Education Project

For a number of years preceding 1981 Professor Günter Biemer of the Catholic Theology Faculty at the University of Freiburg was engaged in a research project investigating the relationship between Judaism and Christianity as it is reflected in German Catholic religious education. It was a major project involving the work of a team of professors, younger scholars, teachers, doctoral and master's students. Master's and doctoral and post-doctoral theses have already been produced within the project, and major guidelines on how Judaism and its relationship to Christianity are to be handled in religious education have appeared.[14] Given the positive and thoroughgoing character of the Guidelines, they doubtless will have a substantial positive effect on Catholic teaching about Judaism.

Scholarship

In a 1978 essay the Catholic scholar Hans Hermann Henrix noted that, "The theme Judaism, to my knowledge, is not included in the lectures and seminars of professors of ecumenical theology. Christian-Jewish questions are rarely handled in dissertations done under the direction of teachers of ecumenical theology. There are few essays devoted to Christian-Jewish relations in German scholarly ecumenical periodical literature."[15]

Interest in Jewish-Christian dialogue is beginning to stir, however, among scholars and university theologians, although there has been relatively little leadership from systematic theologians. Hans Küng and Johannes Metz have been the only two major Catholic systematic theologians to deal significantly with the subject. Leadership for the most part has come from some Scripture scholars, such as Joseph Blank of Saarbrücken, but most of all from Franz Mussner of

Regensburg. Besides his work on the Bishops' Committee discussed above, he has published many scholarly articles in the area, and in 1979 published his 400-page magnum opus, Tractate on the Jews.

Major leadership also comes from Professor Clemens Thoma, a Catholic scholar of Judaism from Lucerne, Switzerland, who wrote an extremely important book, Christian Theology of Judaism (New York: Paulist Press, 1980). A long-time focus for Catholic--and Protestant and Jewish--scholarship on the dialogue is the annual, Freiburger Rundbrief, founded after the war by Dr. Gertrude Luckner and Dr. Karl Thieme, and now continued by Dr. Luckner, who in the Rundbrief essentially edits a major book of essays and documentation each year. Two other Catholic scholars must be mentioned: Hans Hermann Henrix and Walter Strolz. Henrix has written a number of important essays and edited several books dealing with Jewish-Christian dialogue in connection with his work at the Catholic Conference Center at Aachen. Strolz has done similar work in connection with the Catholic publishing house Herder Verlag, which sponsors scholarly conferences on interreligious dialogue and publishes the resulting essays.

Catholic Academies

There are twenty-four Catholic Academies, major conference centers, in West Germany. In the early 1970's, under the leadership of Henrix, the Aachen Academy pioneered conferences on Jewish-Christian relations. In recent years other academies, notably at Wallbeberg, Munich and Hamburg, but others as well, have conducted an increasing number and variety of conferences dealing with one aspect or another of Jewish-Christian relations. In 1979 a new Catholic institute was founded in Munich specifically to promote research and conferences on the relationship between mission and interreligious dialogue, with the promotion of dialogue as its cornerstone. The Chairperson is Professor Heinrich Fries, a long-time Professor of Ecumenical Theology at the Universities of Tübingen and Munich, now emeritus.[16] These dozens of conferences have begun to reach out to the broader ranks of opinion-makers, thereby carrying out the urging of the "Workshop on Jews and Christians." "Jewish-Christian dialogue may no longer be left to the interest of a few specialists. The themes deal with the center of Christian as well as Jewish self-understanding. Furthermore, beyond the encounter between Jews and Christians, they have something essential to contribute to the understanding of all religions and to the future questions of humanity."[17]

Seminarians and Students

Since the early 1970's some Catholic and Protestant seminarians have had the opportunity to spend a year's study in Jerusalem. This is in additon to the numerous shorter study trips to Israel made by a growing number of seminarians and other Catholic and Protestant students, and in addition to the work in kibbutzim and elsewhere in Israel which many German students do through Action Reconciliation (Akzion Zünezeichen).

Oberammergau Passion Play

A final manifestation of the new German Catholic openness and sensitivity to Judaism and Jewish-Christian dialogue relates to the developments in the Oberammergau Passion Play. Every ten years for the past 350 years, this little Alpine village fifty miles south of Munich has been putting on its Passion Play which reflected the antisemitism of the general Christian tradition. After the Holocaust and Vatican II there were attempts made, particularly under the leadership of Rabbi Marc Tannenbaum of the American Jewish Committee (AJC), to eliminate the antisemitic elements from the play for its 1970 production, but to little avail. In 1977 efforts by the AJC and the Anti-Defamation League of B'nai B'rith led by Theodore Freedman to modify the 1980 production were initially met with rebuff. In 1978, however, Mayor Ernst Zwink of Oberammergau told the ADL that he would welcome an analysis of the play by Catholic scholars for antisemitic elements. Leonard Swidler and Gerard Sloyan, two American Catholic scholars, undertook this for the ADL, and their report and suggestions for revision were submitted to the Oberammergau authorities. The text revision, completed in June, 1979, accepted 80% of the suggestions made.[18] Then, in an interview with Swidler and ADL leadership after the May 18, 1980, premiere, Mayor Zwink discussed further revisions and requested that the ADL submit its additional suggestions in writing so that they could be utilized in preparing the 1984 production (350th anniversary year).[19] From hard-line resistance to collaboration in three years! This, too, is part of the extraordinary openness to Jewish-Christian dialogue in contemporary Germany.

In 1981, Bishop Karl Flügel's Committee for Catholic-Jewish Affairs of the German Bishops' Conference, under the leadership of Professor Franz Mussner, was asked by Cardinal Joseph Ratzinger, then Archbishop of Munich, to carry out a study of the text of the Oberammergau Passion Play for any anti-Judaic elements and to make corrective suggestions. This was done, fundamentally endorsing the suggestions of Judith Banki of the American Jewish Committee and Leonard Swidler and Gerard Sloyan, working under the auspices of the Anti-Defamation League. The Bishops' Committee added a number of its own suggestions. The task was completed early in 1982, but just then Cardinal Ratzinger was transferred to Rome and the see of Munich remained vacant for a number of months. Late in 1982 it was filled by Archbishop Friedrich Wetter, who in the spring of the following year encouraged Bishop Flügel and Professor Mussner to meet with the Oberammergau leadership to negotiate the additional improvements. That meeting took place on May 5, 1983.

Unfortunately only a few improvements resulted from that meeting. After the opening performances of the 1984 "season" in May, 1984, extensive and intensive meetings took place between the ADL interreligious delegation and the Oberammergau authorities as well as Bishop Flügel, Professor Mussner and Archbishop Wetter. These produced an agreement to set up a dialogue structure on an ongoing basis to discuss and resolve the remaining problems. Participants in the dialogues would be delegations from America, from the Catholic German Bishops' Conference, and from Oberammergau. In preparation for these further dialogues Swidler and Sloyan produced another small book incorporating their suggested changes, and documentation (The Passion of the Jew Jesus. New York: Anti-Defamation League, 1984).

PROTESTANT ACTIVITIES

Protestant Statements

Since 1964 the Lutheran World Federation, with which a large portion of the German Protestant churches are affiliated, has made a series of positive statements concerning Judaism. Similar statements had already been made by the World Council of Churches in

Amsterdam, 1948; Evanston, 1954; and New Delhi, 1961. In 1950, at Berlin-Weissensee the Protestant Church in Germany, the EKD, confessed its complicity and guilt vis-à-vis the Jews as follows: "We confess before the merciful God that through inaction and silence we shared in the guilt, in the evil committed by members of our nation against the Jews."[20] It was only in 1975, however, that the EKD issued a positive statement on Judaism. The statement, "Christians and Jews: A Study by the Council of the EKD," was quite lengthy (8,500 words) and forward-looking. Its purpose was to assist members of the EKD to rethink their relationship to Jews and "to foster the meeting of Christians and Jews." In 1979, the President of the EKD Council wrote that "Happily since that time both have taken place in great measure. The Study received significant attention from Protestants . . . and has stimulated intensive further theological work, often in common with Catholics."[21]

The EKD Study spoke forthrightly about the complicity of the Christian churches in the Holocaust:

> Only a few Germans had full knowledge of the entire plan of destruction, but most of them knew of the legislation and public Jew-baiting since 1933, the burning of synagogues and plundering of stores in November, 1938, and the sudden disappearance of Jewish neighbors and school fellows. Rumors and foreign news broadcasts also added to the available information. . . . The Christian churches were largely silent. Only a few people at the risk of their own life helped Jews to flee or hid them. . . . From these culpable omissions there arises for us Christians in Germany the special obligation to fight the newly developing antisemitism, even in the form of politically and socially motivated "anti-Zionism," and to collaborate in the forming of a new relationship to Jews.[22]

The study also spoke positively of the State of Israel, a subject which has not been treated by the German Catholic Bishops' Statement or by the Vatican

50

but has been the subject of statements by the Dutch, French and American Catholic bishops. In commenting on the Near East the study carefully stated that Christians are "obligated to recognize and support the internationally valid 1947 U.N. Resolution establishing the State of Israel," and at the same time to "work for an appropriate resolution of the justified claims of both the Palestinian Arabs and the Jews." The study also took a cautious step toward Jewish-Christian-Muslim Trialogue when it stated, "Another important task, despite all evident difficulties, must be the joint effort of Christians, Jews and Muslims on behalf of justice and peace in the Near East."[23]

A few years earlier the World Council of Churches, speaking of "Jews, Christians, and Muslims belonging together spiritually," recommended that "tripartite conversations among Christians, Jews, and Muslims should be organized." In fact these Trialogues have been going on for several years now in several Protestant and Catholic Academies.[24]

The EKD also published a "Workbook" to facilitate its study. This 288-page book was produced in 1979 under the chairmanship of Professor Rolf Rendtorff. It consists of a series of commentaries on every line of the study, with bibliographical and other aids included. It is a first-rate critical scholarship made plain and pertinent to contemporary Christians (see note 21).

In January, 1980, a further significant step was taken when the Synod of the Protestant Church of the Rhineland (a territorial church of the EKD) issued a Declaration "Toward Renewal of the Relationship of Christians and Jews." In it the church "confessed the co-responsibility and guilt of German Christendom for the Holocaust," spoke of the "permanent election of the Jewish people as the people of God" and the realization "that through Jesus Christ the church is taken into the covenant of God with God's people." It went on to state that "the church may not express its witness toward the Jewish people as it does its mission to the peoples of the world." The Declaration also took several concrete actions, such as making provision for the appointment of a permanent church officer responsible for relations with Jews, setting up a permanent committee on cooperation with Jews in which Jews are invited to participate, establishing a seminary chair of Theology, Philosophy, and History of Jewry, and launching a general education campaign concerning relationship with Jews and Judaism.[25]

This Rhineland Synodal Declaration did not, however, go without challenge. In August, 1980, thirteen professors from the Protestant theological faculty of the University of Bonn issued a ten-point critique. The whole tone of the Bonn critique, however, strikes one as quite negative and petty.

Fortunately this challenge did not go unanswered. The Protestant theological faculty of the University of Heidelberg issued a statement on the Bonn critique, severely criticizing it and supporting the Rhineland Declaration. The Heidelbergers saw the Bonn critique as "a regression behind the 'Stuttgart Declaration of Guilt' of 1945 and the 'Statement of Guilt vis-à-vis Israel' of the Synod of the EKD at Berlin-Weissensee in 1950." In defense of the Rhineland Declaration they wrote: "The Synod rightly rejects the 'substitution theory,' according to which 'the New People of God' [i.e., the Church] is understood as a replacement for the 'Old People of God.'" In rejecting the Bonn position on the mission to the Jews, the Heidelbergers affirmed that "The Jews are called to be a light to the Gentiles. In the messianic fulfillment of this mission of Israel those very ones who have been called from among the Gentiles have succeeded in its mission toward the world. From this there does not follow that there is for them any mission toward the Jews."[26]

This debate among Protestant Christians continues. On June 3, 1983, a statement was issued by the leaders of the United Evangelical Lutheran Church of Germany (VELKD) on Jewish-Christian relations which ran in the same direction as the Rhineland Declaration, though not as penetrating. Nevertheless, it confessed "co-responsibility and guilt" for the Holocaust and regretted the churches' silence. In May, 1984, another Synod of the EKD, that of Baden, also issued a Declaration in strong support and imitation of the Rhineland Declaration, likewise confessing co-responsibility and guilt for the Holocaust and affirming a partnership with Judaism in sharing God's revelation and commission to collaborate in building toward the Reign of God on earth.

The strongest German Protestant statement came from the Reformed Alliance in 1984 in commemoration of the 1934 Barmen Declaration of the "Confessing Church" in opposition to Nazism. One German Protestant theologian reported that "these theses already go much further than the Rhineland Declaration. They are substantially more open in their formulation and venture boldly to the roots of the Christian faith, led by the spirit of 'encounter and reconciliation,' determined not to give ground to Christian theology in areas where it has sinned." Thesis one stated that "Christians cast into the Gentile world the seeds of hatred toward the Jews which has wrought destruction and murder. This tradition has not lost its effectiveness and remains evident in the Church and its theology even today." Remarking that still more resolutions from other synods may well be forthcoming, the Protestant theologian Wolfgang Gerlach from Essen warns that "the path to a new understanding might be a century of wandering through the desert and that one must expect to encounter the desire of many to return to the fleshpots of anti-Judaism, to which Paul, John, the Church Fathers and Luther each have contributed ingredients."[27]

Education Project

Headquartered at the University of Duisburg in the industrial Ruhr Valley and under the general inspiration of Professor Heinz Kremers (an Old Testament scholar) is a massive international research and publication project dealing with the history and religion of Judaism entitled: "Jews, Judaism and the State of Israel in West German Textbooks." This is an interdisciplinary project dealing with the humanities, social sciences and pedagogy, including: history, political science, religious education, German, English, geography, and Jewish studies. Collaborators come from various German, Israeli, Belgium and Dutch universities and institutions. The project includes three major research studies analyzing the presentation of Jews, Judaism and the State of Israel in all the history, political science and Protestant religious education textbooks used at present in West Germany. All three studies are funded by the Federal German government. A number of books have already been produced by members of this research team and more are scheduled to follow.[28] In addition, a number of graduate student research projects (Diplomarbeiten and Staatsexamensarbeiten) are also systematically analyzing the presentation of Judaism in textbooks, catechisms, etc. Beyond that is a mushrooming body of learned articles by these scholars on kindred subjects.[29] All together they are building a momentum for change in the teaching about Jews and Judaism by administrators, teachers, and textbook publishers.

Scholarship

In recent years there has been an extraordinary increase in publications by German Protestant theologians which deal positively with Jews and Judaism. Professor Kremers has been extremely active not only in writing his own books[30] but also editing a series of publications, such as "Investigations for Jewish-Christian Dialogue."[31] Since 1976 the Institute for Church and Judaism (Institut Kirche und Judentum) in association with the Protestant Theological University of Berlin (Kirchliche Hochschule Berlin) has published two series of books dealing with different aspects of Jewish-Christian relations. The editor of these series, Peter von der Osten-Sacken, is Professor of New Testament, Director of the Institute, former Rector of the Hochshule, and a prolific scholar.[32] Two dozen books and monographs have already been published in the Institute series! Some of the outstanding German Protestant theologians publishing in this area include: Helmut Gollwitzer, Friedrich Wihelm Marquardt, Rolf Rendtorff, Markus Barth, Martin Stöhr, Jürgen Moltmann, Eberhard Bethge, and Bertold Klappert.

Universities and Students

A small but growing number of lecture courses and seminars is offered at Protestant theological faculties of the universities and seminaries that deal positively with Jewish-Christian relations with a resultant number of graduate-student research projects and doctoral dissertations; the same is true of Catholic theological faculties. In 1979-80 the Religion Department of Temple University, Philadelphia, PA, conducted a year-long seminar on Jewish-Christian dialogue with nine German universities and three academies. The participation on the German side varied from minimal through very intense involvement. Thirteen graduate students, (six Jews, four Catholics and three Protestants) plus four professors (one Protestant, one Jewish and two Catholics) from Temple University met every week, delivered and/or attended a series of thirteen German-language lectures on Jewish-Christian dialogue, produced research papers which were sent to the participating German universities, and critiqued the research papers sent from Germany. At the end of the academic year the seventeen Americans went to Germany for eight weeks of intense dialogue at the twelve universities and academies. Scores of German theology students and professors, Protestant and Catholic, were deeply influenced by the experience. One further result of the project was the publication of a Special Issue of the _Journal of Ecumenical Studies_ entitled _From Holocaust to Dialogue_ (edited by Leonard Swidler, XVIII, 1, Winter, 1981--this Special Issue was generously subsidized by the ADL). A German translation of it is forthcoming. Another result has been the exchange of students and faculty. To date one Dutch and twenty-five German students have come to Temple University's Religion Department to study interreligious dialogue, and ten from Temple have gone to Germany. An exchange of faculty between Temple University and Tübingen University began in 1982, and one in 1983 with Hamburg University. In May, 1984, a second Jewish-Christian dialogue seminar from the Religion Department of Temple University traveled to East Germany for dialogues with seminaries and universities--which among other things produced this volume-- and a similar one in March, 1986.[33]

Protestant Academies

For a number of years, through a wide variety of conferences, Catholic conference centers, and their Protesant counterpart, the Protesant Academies, have been doing yeoman's service in translating the theological advances in Jewish-Christian dialogue on to more practical levels in the lives of Christians. Pastor Martin Stöhr, Director of the Protestant Academy at Arnoldshain, much like Hans Hermann Henrix of the Catholic Academy of Aachen, pioneered such conferences several years ago, oftentimes in collaboration with the Catholic Academy of Aachen. The Berlin Protestant Academy under the leadership of Dr. Franz von Hammerstein (who, like many Germans of the Resistance, spent time in Nazi concentration camps) has also been extraordinarily active in this regard. And because there are 100,000 Muslim workers mostly from Turkey in West Berlin, von Hammerstein has also promoted the Trialogue. Jewish-Christian dialogue seminars, with members of Temple University's Religion Department were held at six such Protestant and Catholic centers in 1980 and four in 1984.

Further specifics both on national and local grass-roots (in East Germany) levels are found in the essays by Werner Vogler and Johannes Hildebrandt in this volume.

JEWISH ACTIVITIES

As noted above, there today are about 28,000 Jews living in Germany, all but a few hundred of whom live in West Germany. This is all that is left of the once flourishing German-Jewish community of over a half million before the advent of the Nazis. Today's German-Jewish community, largely the remnants of the Holocaust, originates from all over Europe. There is a small but increasing number of younger Jews. The community is slowly but clearly reestablishing itself in West Germany.

Besides trying to live its own life and being relatively open to relations with friendly Christians, the German-Jewish community is making two major contributions to Jewish-Christian dialogue today. The first is through a number of important Jewish religious scholars who for years have entered into serious dialogue with Christians on all levels--and the pace is increasing. The most important of these Jewish scholars are Shalom Ben-Chorin, Pinchas Lapide, Peter Levinson, Hans Joachim Schoeps and Ernst L. Erlich. Ben-Chorin, who was raised in Munich before the war, has had a great influence in Germany in recent years through both his lectures and his writings. Until his health began to weaken, he was an immensely popular lecturer. I well remember when I was at the University of Tübingen in 1973 how the largest lecture hall was overfilled with standing-room-only long before Ben-Chorin was scheduled to arrive. When he came in somewhat breathlessly, having just been fetched from the airport, he reported that his manuscript, along with the rest of his luggage, had been misplaced, and so we were asked to bear with his extemporaneous remarks. He then proceeded to deliver an hour-and-a-half-long spell-binding lecture that brought him a well-deserved standing ovation. A prolific writer of both scholarly and popular articles, Ben-Chorin's most important publications have been his trilogy of books: Brother Jesus, Paul and Mother Mary.[34]

The most influential Jewish writer in Germany today is probably Pinchas Lapide. Like Ben-Chorin, Lapide is a Judaica scholar who has also made himself into a very creative New Testament scholar. Lapide was born in Austria, became an Israeli, spent many years after the war living in Israel, but about nine years ago came back to Germany to live and devote himself full time to Jewish-Christian dialogue. He lectures all over the country and has written many articles and over a dozen books dealing in extraordinarily creative ways with different aspects of the Jewish-Christian dialogue.[35]

Mention should also be made of the very important contribution to Jewish-Christian dialogue in Germany being made by other German-born Jews who frequently lecture in Germany. These include David Flusser, New Testament scholar, and Shmaryahu Talmon, a Professor of Hebrew Bible, both from the Hebrew University in Jerusalem. But there are also a number of others.

The second major Jewish contribution to Jewish-Christian dialogue in Germany is the Institute of Higher Jewish Learning (Hochschule für Jüdische Studien) at the University of Heidelberg, established largely through the efforts of Professor Rolf Rendtorff, Old Testament Professor at Heidelberg, whose Rector is Professor Shmaryahu Talmon. Classes started in 1979 and have been expanding ever since. It promises to have a significant influence in the future.

CONCLUSION

It appears evident that in less than one decade there has been an extraordinary flowering of Jewish-Christian dialogue in the land of Heine and the Holocaust. There has been a fundamental shift from diatribe to dialogue. This is not to say that all antisemitism has been eliminated in Germany--any more than it has been in "the land of the free and the home of the brave." It took many centuries to be engendered; it will take at least decades to be completely expelled. To be sure, there will be setbacks, as occurred in the summer of 1982 with the reaction to the Israeli invasion of Lebanon. But the radical Copernican turn has been taken. The Christian religious forces which largely created antisemitism and fostered it over centuries are now fundamentally committed to eliminating it--and more. The creative Christian theological thinkers want to replace it with a positive appreciation of and dialogue with Jews. In this the Germans are joining the creative forces elsewhere in the Christian world and are making their own special contribution.

[1] "Hirtenwort der deutschen Bischöfe vom 23. August 1945," and "Entschliessung des 72. Deutschen katholikentages in Mainz 1948," in Klemens Richter, ed., Die katholische Kirche und das Judentum (Frankfurt: Deutsches Pax-Christi Sekretariat, 1981), p. 29.

[2] "Hirtenwort der deutschen Bischöfe vom 29. August 1962," ibid., p. 30.

[3] "Für ein neues Verhältnis zur Glaubensgeschichte des jüdischen Volkes," ibid., p. 41.

[4] "Erklärung der Delegiertenversammlung der Pax Christi zum 40. Jahrestag der 'Reichskristallnacht,'" ibid., p. 42.

[5] "Stellungnahme des Bensberger Kreises zur Erklärung des Sekretariats der Deutschen Bischofskonferenz 'Die katholische Kirche und der Nationalsozialismus,'" ibid., p. 49.

[6] "Theologische Schwerpünkte des jüdisch-christlichen Gesprächs," ibid., p. 54.

[7] Klemens Richter, "Die katholische Kirche und die Juden," ibid., p. 6.

[8] "Theologische Schwerpünkte des jüdische-christlichen Gesprächs," ibid., pp. 55, 57.

[9] Franz Mussner, Traktate über die Juden (Munich: Kosel Verlag, 1979). English translation and introduction by Leonard Swidler, Tractate on the Jews (Philadelphia, Fortress Press, 1984).

[10] "Über das Verhältnis der Kirche zum Judentum," Richter, Die katholische Kirche und das Judentum, p. 71.

[11] Ernst Ludwig Ehrlich, "Katholiken im Gespräch mit Juden," ibid., p. 28.

[12] Erich Zenger, "Der Dialog muss weitergehen," ibid., p. 17.

[13] Tommaso Federici, "Study Outline on the Mission and Witness of the Church," Sidic, XI, 3 (1978), pp. 25-34.

[14] Cf. Peter Fiedler, Das Judentum im katholischen Religionsunterricht (Düsseldorf: Patmos, 1980). Günter Biemer, Freiburger Leitlinien zum Lernprozess Christen Juden (Düsseldorf: Patmos, 1981).

[15] Hans Hermann Henrix, "Ökumene aus Juden und Christen. Ein theologischer Versuch," in H. Henrix and M. Stohr, eds., Exodus und Kreuz im ökumenischen Dialog zwischen Juden und Christen (Aachen: Einhard Verlag, 1978), pp. 190-191.

[16] The Director of the new institute, the Katholisches Institut für Missionstheologische Grundlagenforschung, is Dr. Franz Wolfinger, Pettenkoferstr. 26, Munich 2. The Institute has already published two books: Jesus in den Weltreligionen and Heil in den Religionen und im Christentum.

[17] "Theologische Schwerpünkte des jüdisch-christlichen Gesprächs," p. 59.

[18] Leonard Swidler and Gerard S. Sloyan, A Commentary on the Oberammergau Passionsspiel in Regard to Its Image of Jews and Judaism (New York: Anti-Defamation League, 1978).

[19] Leonard Swidler, ed., The Oberammergau Passionsspiel 1984 (New York: Anti-Defamation League, 1980).

[20] Quoted in Karl-Joseph Kuschel, "Ecumenical Consensus on Judaism in Germany?" Journal of Ecumenical Studies, XX, 3 (Summer, 1983), p. 387.

[21] D. Class, "Vorwort," in Rolf Rendtorff, ed., Arbeitsbuch Christen und Juden (Gütersloh: Gerd Mohn, 1979), p. 9.

[22] "Christians and Jews. A Study by the Council of the Evangelical Church in Germany," in Helga Kroner, ed., Stepping Stones to Further Jewish-Christian Relations (London: Stimulus Books, 1977), p. 145.

[23] Ibid., p. 146.

[24] Jewish-Christian Dialogue (Geneva: International Jewish Committee on Interreligious Consultations and the World Council of Churches' Sub-Unit on Dialogue with People of Living Faiths and Ideologies, 1975), p. 11.

[25] English in JES, XVII, 1 (Winter, 1980), pp. 211f.

[26] Citations in Kuschel, "Ecumenical Consensus."

[27] Wolfgang Gerlach, "Did Protestants in Germany Learn Their Lessons from History?" a lecture delivered on March 11, 1985, in Philadelphia, at the fifteenth annual Scholar's Conference on the Holocaust and Church Struggle cosponsored by the National Conference of Christians and Jews, founded and organized by Professor Franklin Littell of the Religion Department, Temple University.

[28] E.g., Klaus Farber and Heinz Kremers, Juden, ein Beitrag zur Behandlung der Vorurteilsproblematik im Unterricht (Dortmund: W. Cruwell Verlag, 1974); Gerd Stein and E. Horst Schallenberger, eds., Schulbuch Analyse und Schulbuchkritik. Im Brennpunkt: Juden, Judentum und Staat Israel (Duisburg: Verlag der Sozialwissenschaftlichen Kooperative, 1976); Chaim Schatzker, Jüdische Geschichte in deutschen Geschichts- lehrbüchern (Braunschweig: Albert Limbach Verlag, 1963); Chaim Schatzker, Das Deutschland-Bild in israelischen Schulgeschichtsbüchern (Braunschweig: Albert Limbach Verlag, 1979); Herbert Jochum and Heinz Kremers, eds., Juden, Judentum und Staat Israel im christlichen Religionsunterricht in der Bundesrepublik Deutschland (Paderborn: Schöningh, 1980).

[29] For an extensive listing of the pertinent periodical literature produced by these scholars, see the photocopied report, "Pubkilationen und noch unveröffentlichte sowie in Arbeit befindliche Unter- suchungen der Projektgruppe: Juden, Judentum und Staat Israel in Schulbüchern der BRD an der Gesamthochschule Duisburg," 1979. See also the Special Issue of the Journal of Ecumenical Studies, XXI, 3 (Summer, 1984), edited by Judith Banki.

[30] E.g., Heinz Kremers, Judenmission heute? (Neukirchen-Vluyn: Neukirchener Verlag, 1979).

[31] E.g., of the series Forschungen zum jüdisch- christlichen Dialog, edited by Yehuda Aschkenasy and Heinz Kremers (Neukirchen-Vluyn: Neukirchener Verlag). The first volume in the series appeared in 1976: Pinchas Lapide, Hebräisch in den Kirchen.

[32] One of Peter von der Osten-Sacken's latest books is _Grundzüge einer Theologie im christlich-jüdischen Gespräch_ (Munich: Chr. Kaiser Verlag, 1982).

[33] See the introduction of this volume for specifics.

[34] Schalom Ben Chorin, _Bruder Jesus. Der Nazarener in jüdischer Sicht_ (Munich: Paul List Verlag, 1967); _Paulus. Der Völkerapostel in jüdischer Sicht_ (Munich: Paul List Verlag, 1970); _Mutter Mirjam. Maria in jüdischer Sicht_ (Munich: Paul List Verlag, 1971).

[35] E.g., Pinchas Lapide and Hans Küng, _Jesus im Widerstreit. Ein jüdisch-christlicher Dialog_ (Stuttgart-Munich: Calwer-Kösel, 1976); Pinchas Lapide, _Ist das nicht Josephs Sohn? Jesus im heutigen Judentum_ (Stuttgart-Munich: Calwer-Kösel, 1976); Pinchas Lapide, _Juden und Christen_ (Zurich: Benziger, 1976); Pinchas Lapide, _Auferstehung Ein jüdisches Glaubenserlebnis_ (Stuttgart-Munich: Calwer-Kösel, 1977); Pinchas Lapide, Franz Mussner and Ulrich Wilckens, _Was Juden und Christen von einander denken_ (Freiburg: Herder, 1978); Pinchas Lapide and Ulrich Luz, _Der Jude Jesus. Thesen eines Juden. Antworten eines Christen_ (Zurich: Benziger, 1979); Pinchas Lapide and Jürgen Moltmann, _Jüdischer Monotheismus--Christliche Trinitätslehre. Ein Gespräch_ (Munich: Chr. Kaiser, 1979); English translation by Leonard Swidler, _Jewish Monotheism and Christian Trinitarian Doctrine_ (Philadelphia: Fortress Press, 1981); Pinchas Lapide and Carl Friedrich von Weizsäcker, _Die Seligpreisungen. Ein Glaubensgepräch_ (Stuttgart-Munich: Calwer-Kösel, 1980); Pinchas Lapide, _Er predigte in ihren Synagogen. Jüdische Evangelienauslegung_ (Gütersloh: Gerd Mohn, 1980); Pinchas Lapide and Jürgen Moltmann, _Israel und Kirche: ein gemeinsamer Weg? Ein Gespräch_ (Munich: Chr. Kaiser, 1980); Pinchas Lapide and Helmut Gollwitzer, _Ein Flüchtlingskind. Auslegungen zu Lukas 2_ (Munich: Chr. Kaiser, 1981); Pinchas Lapide and Peter Stuhlmacher, _Paulus Rabbi und Apostel. Ein jüdisch-christlicher Dialog_ (Stuttgart-Munich: Calwer-Kösel), 1981); _Die Bergpredigt--Utopie oder Programm?_ (Mainz: Matthias Grünewald Verlag, 1982)--English translation by Arlene Swidler (Orbis Books, 1986); _Jeder kommt zum Vater. Barmen und die Folgen_ (Neukirchen-Vluyn: Neukirchener, 1984).

THE DIALOGUE BETWEEN CHURCH AND SYNAGOGUE

by

Werner Vogler

The dialogue between church and synagogue has in recent years--especially among the young Christians of our land--gained increasing attention. As encouraging as this fact is, it must nevertheless not delude us into forgetting that this dialogue is still pretty much in its initial stage. That is especially clear from the first of the following six sections reporting on this dialogue.

1. The Prevention of a Misunderstanding

Because our topic can be misunderstood, steps must first of all be taken to prevent a possible error. This error would be found in the definite article "the." "The" dialogue between church and synagogue has until now not taken place. And presumably it cannot. And just as there has not been "the" dialogue between church and synagogue, so also until now there has been no dialogue between "the" church and "the" synagogue. For, abstracting from the question of who "the" church and who "the" synagogue really are, until today there have always been only dialogues between individual representatives of the two groups. These representatives were encouraged to participate in such dialogues by one side (church) as well as the other (synagogue). Indeed, they were even often delegated, but they were never authorized in a strict sense, that is, they were never designated as dialogue plenipotentiaries (of any kind). Rather, it was above all their personal involvement that led them to seek each other out in these dialogues.

2. Reasons for This Dialogue

In the "Working Paper of the Dialogue Circle 'Jews and Christians'" published in 1980 two reasons for the carrying out of this dialogue between Jews and Christians were given:

"1. Jews and Christians have a common basis for their hope: the God of Israel who turns graciously toward humanity. They await in common the complete fulfillment of their hope: the final Reign of God.

Jews and Christians are challenged by what they have experienced of God to bear a common witness to the world in which they live. . . . 2. If the obligation to dialogue which is valid for all times lies in the fact that Jews and Christians are bound together in the action of the God of Israel, the experiences so full of suffering in recent history confirm the commission to intensify and deepen this dialogue with all of our powers in our time. . . . Jews and Christians have a common witness to bear to a humanity whose survival as humanity is at stake; as a concrete witness it must show and prepare concrete ways of justice and healing."[1]

The theological reason, given first above, is most significant for the Jewish-Christian dialogue. It permits us to recognize the authentic occasion for this dialogue: God's merciful turning toward Jews and Christians, that is, the opening up of God's fatherhood which was imparted to them, as well as the resultant witness of the two toward the world--bringing it salvation. From there it can be seen as a development of this ground for dialogue when Shalom Ben-Chorin remarked concerning the necessity of dialogue between church and synagogue: "We must come together in dialogue because we are asked about each other. . . . The ancient covenant exists, and the new covenant exists. The ancient and new covenants have not dissolved each other, but rather they persist through time. And since it is the case that the covenants really exist, the bearers of the covenant are asked from the perspective of the existence of one about the existence of the other. . . . And further, we recognize ourselves more clearly and more deeply in the mirror of the other."[2] Thus the church must ask: "How has Israel understood its Holy Scripture?" And the synagogue must ask: "How has the church interpreted this message which came to it from Israel? We should learn from one another, even learn from the errors which here and there were committed."[3] It is certain that "the difference in the commission is clearly stated. The Christian stands under an immediate mission command, while a Jew stands only under the commission to bear witness to God." Nevertheless, it cannot be doubted that "the message which we both have to deliver, Jews and Christians, lead us to one another."[4] All this is doubtless correctly stated. Further, the possibility is not to be seriously entertained that there could be Jews or Christians who could continuously close themselves off

64

to what here has been said without thereby becoming guilty in their being Jews or being Christians.

3. The Way of Dialogue between Church and Synagogue

If one excepts the efforts of the Leipzig Old Testament scholar F. Delitzsch concerning Judaism--in the sense of the 19th-century mission to the Jews which was initiated by him--the dialogue between church and synagogue first began after the First World War. It has two roots. On the one hand it began on an organizational level when in 1928 at the conference of the International Mission Council in Jerusalem a "Committee for the Christian Mission to the Jews" was established (from this after the incorporation of the International Mission Council into the World Council of Churches the "Consultation of the Church and the Jewish People" developed). On the other hand it took concrete form as two Jews and two Christians--the avant-garde on both sides--took up the dialogue with each other on German soil. However, this dialogue came to a very early (temporary) close in the noteworthy disputation which M. Buber held with the Protestant New Testament scholar K. L. Schmidt in Stuttgart on January 14, 1933--only a few days before Hitler seized power.[5] And with that for the time being the possibilities were also destroyed which Martin Buber expressed there in view of the future encounter of Jews and Christians: "In all this what binds together Jews and Christians is their common knowledge of a single thing, and from that we can reach across the deepest divide to each other; every genuinely sacred thing can acknowledge the mystery of another genuinely sacred thing. The mystery of the other is within and cannot be perceived from without. No person outside of Israel knows of the mystery of Israel. And no person outside of Christianity knows of the mystery of Christianity. But even not knowing, we can acknowledge each other in the mystery. How it is possible that there are mysteries alongside of each other is God's mystery. How it is possible that there is a world as a house in which these mysteries dwell together is God's concern, for the world is God's house. It is not because we question anyone concerning the reality of his or her faith; it is not that we wish by some subterfuge to introduce collaboration despite differences, but rather it is because with the acknowledgment of the differences that we share with each other in unconditioned trust what we know of the unity of this house. We hope that we one day will feel ourselves filled with its unity, without

65

walls of division around us. We serve divided from and yet with one another, until one day we will be united in a common service, until we all will, as it says in the Jewish prayer on the feast of the new year: 'Be a single covenant for the sake of doing his will.'"[6]

After the Second World War the dialogue between Jews and Christians which had been broken off between 1933 to 1945 began relatively quickly again. That was not suprising when one recalls that in the years of violent National Socialist domination Jews and Christians came very close to each other as fellow oppressed. Nevertheless, on the Jewish side there were also some hesitations about the continuance of the dialogue. Thus, for example, the American Jew E. Berkovits raised the following objection: "We reject the idea of interreligious understanding as immoral because it is an attempt to whitewash a criminal past."[7] Because for Berkovits the Holocaust of National Socialism was understandable only against the background of the centuries-long anti-Jewish polemic of Christianity, his only demand of Christians was "that they keep their hands off us and our children."[8] This reaction--even though understandable--nevertheless, is not typical. The relationship between Christian anti-Judaism and National Socialistic antisemitism is not seen by most Jews of our day quite so undialectically as is the case with Berkovits. Rather, from the Jewish side the stress was much more that Christianity in the face of the events of Auschwitz is urgently in need of a self-analysis. In this it is doubtless rightly recognized that the so-called "final solution" of the Jewish question, which in the years of National Socialism was connected with the name of Auschwitz-- which also stands for all the other death camps of this time--presents the greatest challenge to the church and its theology.

The dialogue between Jews and Christians which began again after the war's end led to one between individually distinguished dialogue partners (mostly theologians) of both groups. On the Jewish side, after Martin Buber, the following should be mentioned first of all: L. Baeck, R. R. Geis, H. L. Goldschmidt, H.-J. Schoeps, as well as S. Ben-Chorin, E. L. Ehrlich, D. Flusser, P. Lapide and N. Levinson. On the Christian side they are, after K. L. Schmidt, especially K. Barth, H. Grüber, K. H. Rengstorf, as well as H.-J. Kraus, H. Küng, F. Mussner, R. Rendtorff, P. v. d. Osten-Sacken and C. Thoma. In another sphere (and closely related with these just-mentioned encounters) the dialogue took, and takes, place between church and synagogue since the end of World War II on various levels, including the following:

1. The "Working Circle of Church and Judaism of the United Evangelical-Lutheran Church of Germany" (VELKD). This group has existed since 1968 and represents on the Evangelical-Lutheran side the "lowest" level of the encounter between Jews and Christians. Corresponding to it in the German Democratic Republic is the "Working Community Church and Judaism," or "Working Community Judaism and Christianity," of which there are until now three (in Leipzig, Berlin and Dresden). Its task consists mainly in that through it Christians learn to know and understand Judaism, since a dialogue with Judaism is here--because of extremely small synagogue congregations--for all practical purposes not possible. It is different in West Germany. There this dialogue is carried on in a series of supraregional working circles. Among these are included the "Working Community Jews and Christians at the German Protestant Church Day," the "Study Commission 'Church and Judaism' of the Evangelical Church in Germany," the "Working Group Christians and Jews," the "German Coordinating Council of the Society for Christian-Jewish Collaboration," as well as the "Conference of the Provincial Churches' Working Circles Church and Israel."

2. Another ("middle") level of encounter between Jews and Christians is represented by the "consultations," which are sponsored by the study division of the Lutheran World Federation (in Geneva). Until now four such "consultations" (that is, conferences of several days' length) have taken place: 1964 in Logumkloster (topic: The Church and the Jewish People), 1973 in Neuendettelsau (with a continuation of the topic from Logumkloster), 1975 in Oslo (topic: Christian Witness and the Jewish People), and 1982 in Bossey (topic: The Significance of Judaism for the Life and Mission of the Church). The (about 50) participants at these meetings were Lutherans from all over the world and representatives of Judaism.

3. The ("highest") level of the presently conducted Jewish-Christian dialogues are the "consultations" (which have taken place regularly since 1965) between representatives of the World Council of Churches and the Jewish world organizations which at

67

the initiative of the Jewish World Congress have jointly constituted the "International Jewish Committee for Interreligious Consultations." This "Committee" handles all negotiations with the World Council of Churches and the confessional world organizations as well as with the Vatican. Representatives of all the churches take part in these "consultations" so that here the presupposition and the foundation for later encounters on the confessional level are created. These include the consultations between the representatives of the International Jewish Committee for Interreligious Consultations and the Lutheran World Federation (about 25 participants), of which two have taken place so far: 1981 in Copenhagen (topic: The Concept of the Human Being in the Lutheran and Jewish Traditions), and 1983 in Stockholm (topic: Luther, Lutheranism and the Jews).

In this connection the Jewish-Christian dialogue conducted with the Roman Catholic Church should be noted. The impulse for this was given by Pope John XXIII. It was begun, however, through the Second Vatican Council on the basis of Article 4 of the Conciliar Declaration "Nostra Aetate" ("Declaration on the Relationship of the Church to Non-Christian Religions") passed on December 1, 1964.[9] This dialogue is carried on at present above all through the "Dialogue Circle 'Jews and Christians' of the Central Committee of German Catholics."[10]

Until now there has been no comprehensive presentation of the dialogue between church and synagogue that has taken place since 1945.[11] However, there are--on various levels--a number of publication organs on Jewish-Christian dialogue. Among these above all the following are to be mentioned: the newsletter of the Christian-Jewish working community, "Christlich-Jüdisches Forum," published in Basel; the magazine, likewise published in Switzerland, Judaica, along with its occasional Beiträge zum Verständnis des jüdischen Schicksals in Vergangenheit und Gegenwart; the "Publishing Series for Christian-Jewish Encounter" published in Wuppertal; as well as the periodical published by Catholic theologians, Freiburger Rundbrief.

4. The Content of This Dialogue

The dialogue between church and synagogue after 1945 was characterized primarily by three elements desired on the Jewish side: 1. What guarantees can Christians give for the elimination of antisemitism as it has been known in the history of Christianity? (From here there developed the theme of "anti-Judaism in the New Testament," which subsequently has taken on an increasing significance.[12]) 2. In what way can Christians identify with the right of the Jewish people to their own Jewish state? 3. What assurances can Christians give against Jewish conversions' being forcibly carried out?

These themes, which were understandable in that situation, have, with the exception of "anti-Judaism in the New Testament," been replaced by other themes which since then have shaped the dialogue between Jews and Christians: 4. The passion of Israel and the passion of Jesus. 5. The "Reign" of God from Jewish and Christian perspectives. 6. The understanding of God by Jews and by Christians. These themes were later still further expanded or supplemented: 7. Jesus and 8. Paul in the understanding of Jews and Christians. 9. Jewish and Christian faith. 10. The meaning of the Torah in the life of Jews and of Christians.

The discussion of these dialogue themes--which in individual cases have also been published[13]--has been enriched in recent years by those topics which were taken up at the Jewish-Christian "consultations" mentioned in section three. Beyond those there were dialogue themes such as: 11. Are there two paths to salvation? Is the Torah valid for Israel and Jesus Christ for the Church? 12. In what sense is the Old Testament of the Christians and the Bible of the Jews the same scripture? 13. Are there common tasks in the world for Jews and Christians? 14. How can Jews and Christians through dialogue be a role model for the worldwide community?

5. The Present Status of the Dialogue between Church and Synagogue

The term "status" in this subheading is not to be so understood as if the following were a kind of definition of the status of the Jewish-Christian dialogue in each of the dialogue themes mentioned in section four. That is not possible. Rather, the term "status" here means an inquiry leading to a general summary of the dialogue between church and synagogue which has taken place to this time. The thus understood description of the position of the Jewish-Christian dialogue shows at present the following results:

1.   The dialogue conducted until now has dismantled mistrust on both sides. That is shown on the Jewish side by the fact that their dialogue partners met with Christians and discussed with them without their fearing that they would be taken in by the Christian side. On the Christian side this dismantling of mistrust is expressed in the fact that the Christian representatives developed the inner freedom to approach their Jewish dialogue partners without feeling forced out of motives of guilt (because of the events of the years 1933-1945).

2.   Each side has come to know the particular manner of the other representatives and has learned to understand them to a degree. Moreover, both sides have in the course of time learned to appreciate each other. This is expressed in the fact that--in a positive sense--the representatives deal with each other with care. Examples here would include the Jewish speaking of the first covenant as over against the second (Christian), and also the Christian references to God as <u>Adonai</u> or <u>Elohim</u>. An especially important example here is the increasing Christian recognition that the Jewish people (despite their rejection of Jesus as the Christ) remain, after as well as before, God's chosen and beloved people.

In this connection it is true to repeat what the participants of the Jewish-Christian "consultation" in November, 1981, in Arnoldshain stated in their preparatory paper for the world assembly of the World Council of Churches in Vancouver (in 1983): "We learned that it is painful truly to listen to others, for then we had to see ourselves and the world through the eyes of others. We learned, to our surprise, that the convictions and traditions which were obvious to us were both placed in question and enriched. Thus we discovered again the biblical experience that faith grows when it is put at stake. We discovered that an encounter with 'strangers' in which they can express themselves in their own words generates a sense of community: a community which retains the tensions which grow out of genuine differences and at the same time provides the experience of unity which stems from that which we have in common. The dialogue has challenged us to a new witness of our faith--toward our partners in dialogue, toward the communities from which we come and toward those whom we have yet to encounter."[14]

3. On the basis of the dialogue which has taken place so far between Jews and Christians there has developed a relationship which one can most accurately describe as a relationship of neighbors. Since, however, there are completely different kinds of neighborhoods, this relationship needs to be more specifically described. The sense of neighborhood that has grown up between Jews and Christians is not one simply of a friendly closeness based merely on mutual respect, or indeed delimitation, but rather it is a sense of neighborhood from encounter, in specific cases, even close partnership.

4. In this sense of neighborliness from the encounter between church and synagogue there is included the fact that Jews and Christians should "be ready always to give an answer to every one that asks a reason for the hope that is in you" (1 Peter 3:15). That is, not only does the Jewish-Christian dialogue, from both sides, exclude the making up to or indeed the "taking in" of the other, but there is also great mutual concern for the acknowledgment of the stance of faith of the other group. Beyond all this, this dialogue is also characterized by the imparting to the other (in the sense stated by Martin Buber in section three above)--and as far as possible, allowing the other to participate in--what belongs to the most valuable heritage of each believing community.

5. The dialogue between church and synagogue until now has shown that Jews and Christians are not only different from one another. They are also characterized by the common content of their faith. This includes in the first order the belief in the one God of Israel, the creator of the world and Ruler of heaven and earth, as well as the hope in the establishment of the escatological salvific sovereignty of our God at the end of this earthly time. From this, however--and we will delve into this more in detail in the next section--there arises for the two communities, despite their differences, a common task: to witness before the world to this God and God's expected sovereignty over the world.

6. The Goal of This Dialogue

The goal of the dialogue between church and synagogue can under no circumstances be perceived to be the
eliminating or ignoring of the differences that exist
between them--and which will also remain in the future.
Instead of this, the words of Shalom Ben-Chorin concerning the goal of the Jewish-Christian dialogue
should be agreed with when he describes it (see above
section two) as a "learning from one another."
"Learning from one another," however, means first of
all being open to others in order to learn to know
them better and thereby to understand them better than
before. "Learning from one another" means, then, the
testing of one's own standpoint against that of the
other. Such a testing, however, can have two different
consequences: it can result in the correction of the
previously held standpoint, or it can mean a confirma-
tion of one's own view. "Learning from one another"
means most of all, however, viewing the others, despite
their different ways, as human beings loved by God, and
gaining from this point forward a new attitude not only
toward them themselves but also toward the community of
which they are members.

A further goal of this dialogue must be seen in
the joint effort of Jews and Christians to testify
before a secularized world to the God who wishes the
salvation of all human beings, to a God who is their
God, and to make this God transparent to them through
joint action. Such transparency can happen first of
all through standing up for greater humaneness, especially there where defective (social) justice or
discriminations and persecutions infringe upon the
lives of human beings. This transparency can further
result through the passing on of peace--as a gift given
to both of them by their God--and not only there where
unpeace or (nuclear) armament immediately threatens the
existence of humanity. This transparency finally will
be made available by dealing with one another in a
model fashion, which will lead to imitation, for in
this way Jews and Christians call attention to their
faith and thereby to their God.

The final goal of the Jewish-Christian dialogue,
and thereby the highest form of consensus between Jews
and Christians, will, however, be the common worship of
the one God by church and synagogue. For such prayer
likewise presumes that it will demonstrate that those
so united have made their being children of God their

own--even if it is imparted to them in different ways. Before reaching this there is, of course, still a further way to go, but the beginning points for such common prayer already lie at hand.[15] Nevertheless, as promising and encouraging as these are, they are of course only beginnings, just as the dialogue between church and synagogue in general is only a beginning dialogue. Despite present difficulties, however, it is a promising and encouraging dialogue for those who have participated in it.

Translated by

Leonard Swidler

[1] Theologisches Jahrbuch (Leipzig, 1980), p. 169.

[2] Possibilities and limitations of the Christian-Jewish dialogue are found in ibid.; see also Shalom Ben-Chorin, "Das Judentum im Ringen der Gegenwart," Evangelische Zeitstimmen (Hamburg-Bergstedt, 1965), 22/23, pp. 30f.

[3] Ibid., pp. 40f.

[4] Ibid., p. 33.

[5] This dialogue has been printed several times, most recently in K. L. Schmidt, Neues Testament-Judentum-Kirche. Kleine Schriften--Theologische Bücherei, vol. 69 (Munich, 1981), pp. 149-165. The written record of the total dialogue between church and synagogue up to the year 1933 is found in R. R. Geis and H.-J. Kraus, eds., Versuche des Verstehens. Dokumente jüdisch-christlicher Begegnung aus den Jahren 1918-1933. Theologische Bücherei, vol. 33 (Munich, 1966).

[6] Ibid., pp. 159f.

[7] Cited in G. Baumbach, "Der christlich-jüdische Dialog," Die Zeichen der Zeit (Berlin, 1981), p. 173.

[8] Ibid.

[9] In this article the previous teaching of the cursing and the rejection of the Jews by God is likewise declared to be false, and respect, fraternity and dialogue with the Jews is demanded.

[10] This dialogue circle issued on May 8, 1979, "Theologische Schwerpunkte des jüdisch-christlichen Gesprächs," Theologisches Jahrbuch, pp. 169-176.

[11] There are to this point, however, many individual publications, of which two will be referred to here: J. Melzer, ed., Deutsch-jüdisches Schicksal. Wegweiser durch das Schrifttum der letzten 15 Jahre 1945 bis 1960 (Cologne, 1960); H. H. Henrix, "In der Entdeckung von Zeitgenossenschaft. Ein Literaturbericht zum christlich-jüdischen Gespräch der letzten Jahre," Theologisches Jahrbuch, pp. 177-192.

[12] Concerning this see, for example, the volume of collected essays with the same name containing lectures from a study conference for Jewish and Christian theologians (mainly exegetes) which took place in June, 1966, in Arnoldshain: W. Eckert, N. P. Levinson and M. Stöhr, eds., _Abhandlungen zum christlich-jüdischen Dialog_ (Munich, 1967), vol. 2.

[13] Of these some have appeared in print: H. Küng--P. Lapide, _Jesus in Widerstreit. Ein jüdisch-christlicher Dialog_ (Stuttgart-Munich, 1976); P. Lapide--F. Mussner--U. Wilkens, _Was Juden und Christen voneinander denken. Bausteine zum Brückenschlag_ (Freiburg, Basel, Vienna, 1987); P. Lapide--U. Luz, _Der Jude Jesus_ (Zurich-Einsiedeln-Cologne, 1979); P. Lapide--J. Moltmann, _Jüdischer Monotheismus-christliche Trinitätslehre. Ein Gespräch_ (Munich, 1980); P. Lapide--J. Moltmann, _Israel und Kirche: ein gemeinsamer Weg? Ein Gespräch_ (Munich, 1980); P. Lapide--C. F. von Weizsäcker, _Die Seligpreisungen. Ein Glaubensgespräch_ (Stuttgart-Munich, 1980); P. Lapide--W. Pannenberg, _Judentum und Christentum. Einheit und Unterschied_ (Munich, 1981); P. Lapide--P. Stuhlmacher, _Paulus, Rabbi und Apostel. Ein jüdisch-christlicher Dialog_ (Stuttgart-Munich, 1981).

[14] "Juden und Christen unterwegs auf dem Wege nach Vancouver," in duplicated manuscript form by the Bund der Evangelischen Kirchen in der Deutschen Demokratischen Republik, Berlin, n.d., p. 1.

[15] Cf. M. Brocke, J. J. Petuchowski and W. Strolz, eds., _Das Vaterunser Gemeinsames im Beten von Juden und Christen_ (Freiburg, 1974), as well as P. Nave, _Du unser Vater. Jüdische Gebete dür Christen_ (Freiburg, 1975).

JEWISH-CHRISTIAN DIALOGUE:
A GRASS ROOTS REPORT FROM EAST BERLIN

by

Pastor Johannes Hildebrandt

Our Working Group has always been solidly based on the level of the congregation. It receives its life from and is shaped by work at the grass roots. Its small core consists of a working group of members of the congregation of the Protestant church of Saint Sophia in Berlin. This group has added further members from congregations of other Berlin churches and churches around the perimeter of Berlin, as well as nearby cities. We are pleased that our circle also has participants from some other denominations, such as Baptist, Methodist and Catholic. Our Working Group is an assembly of Christians whose goal is to encourage each other and others under the motto, "Everyone can learn to know and understand Judaism and Christianity better if he or she wishes to."

To date we have grown to a circle of around four hundred interested participants, of whom about a hundred attend each of our lecture and discussion sessions. In addition, for special presentations, which we hold in the church of St. Sophia, we can expect substantially more participants, very many of whom are young people.

Our annual program is prepared by a small executive committee. The various programs are carried out in conjunction with the responsible authorities for ecumenical affairs of the Protestant Consistory of Berlin-Brandenburg and also the Speaker for religious affairs of the Jewish community of Berlin.

The goal of our Working Group is to help dismantle prejudices against Judaism in order to be able correctly to encounter the Jewish people, their religion and their state. We were stunned that it was precisely our people--which indeed in its tradition has been a "Christian" people--which was responsible for the Shoah (Holocaust) of the Jews and now must be responsible for it. It is difficult for us to admit that we--even the ones born later!--have become members of a murderous people and belong to a religion which by its history and its claim of absoluteness encouraged, rather than

77

hindered, this incomprehensible mass murder. We wish to come to know Judaism. We wish to ask about the relationship between Judaism and Christianity. We wish to analyze our Christianity critically in regard to its false decisions and erroneous paths in relationship to Judaism. We wish to become conscious of the great degree in which we ourselves are rooted in the Jewish world of belief and are oriented toward its life's values. We discern that our churches not only in the past were unjust toward Judaism, but also in general even today are still not correct in their preaching, church writings, church education and instruction.

In our meetings, which focus on lectures and discussion, we deal with the following areas:

1) _Shoah_ (Holocaust), recalling the events.

2) The history of Israel (from the beginnings to the present).

3) The religion of Judaism (synagogue, customs, literature, hymns, etc.).

4) Interpretation of texts from the Hebrew and Christian Scriptures (Bible).

5) Anti-Jewish and misunderstandable selections of the New Testament.

6) Anti-Judaism, anti-Zionism, anti-Israelism.

7) The Jewish community in Berlin and Berlin local history.

8) The assimilation of the past in regard to the attitude of the generations to one another and the question of the handing on of experiences.

9) Critical reflections on events which can again stimulate the old anti-semitism.

10) Cooperation in the area of practice with the Jewish community in individual cases.

The field is so broad that until now we have not needed to complain about a lack of material. We often have guests among us who help us work through the various topics. The most prominent guest was the Vice President of the Jewish World Congress, Dr. Gerhart Riegner. He visited us early in 1985. We are especially pleased and thankful that the President of the Jewish community of Berlin (East), Dr. Peter Kirchner, and a number of members of the Jewish community help us by lectures and encouragement and suggestions. A large part of the programs, however, are conducted out of our own resources.

Because a large portion of our participants are professionally active or are often traveling, we concentrate our programs to perhaps one every three months in which we bring together several presentations on one working day (afternoon to late evening). That is, of course, demanding for some participants but nevertheless rewarding, because in this manner we are able to penetrate into the whole theme much more deeply and make its concern intensively our own. The various sessions are divided by coffee breaks. In addition to these conference days we also from time to time sponsor individual programs in response to various events and questions raised. On November 9 we annually hold a memorial for the <u>Kristallnacht</u> of 1939 in the church of St. Sophia and afterwards light candles in front of the Oranienburg Street Synagogue, which was damaged by the Nazis and bombed out in World War II, and in front of the memorial on Gross Hamburger Street which was erected to those deported to the death camps.

We occasionally put together working papers for our membership. They are of various sorts. The above-named topics are reflected here again. They are in effect short lectures. One working paper, e.g., dealt with a practical matter: baking recipes for Hamantaschen for the feast of Purim. Another offered comparative synopses of the liturgical structures of the synagogue and the church. In our program we often sing songs from the Jewish tradition in order to remind us clearly that our relationship to Judaism need not be only of a religious sort, but that Judaism wishes to be taken as a whole, that religion and land belong in the "house of Israel." Interested young people and members of our Working Group have also developed two small exhibitions which we can set up in various localities. One of these large placards describes the history of Israel with a special reference to the Berlin situation, and the other is devoted to the Jewish cemetery on Schönhauser Allee.

The various programs of our Working Group are financially supported by the donations of the participants. Of course all services are donated. Even I am fully occupied professionally in my parish pastoral work in the congregation of St. Sophia and can conduct this important work of the Working Group only on the side, to some extent in my free time.

Perhaps a few words concerning the founding of the Working Group are in order. It arose quite spontaneously; it was not planned or organized. Rather, it simply grew out of some lectures and parish seminars. I began in 1975 with several lectures for various church groups. Among other things, I was especially concerned to help clear up misunderstandings which, for example, appeared to be developing from the United Nations resolution of November 11, 1975, in which Zionism was compared with racism. Our efforts to provide a nuanced presentation in the most varied areas were noticed by the church authorities, and we were asked to open up the small Working Group, "Judaism and Christianity," which had in the meanwhile developed out of our small congregational circle, to those interested persons from the whole church area from Berlin-Brandenburg. A year later the Synod of our church, at its annual synodal conference in April, 1981, declared the activity of the Working Group to be "part of the responsibility of reconciliation of the church" and "encouraged the Working Group not to lessen its efforts in the areas of information and understanding" ("Rückschau," Synodal Report, April, 1981, p. 17).

Translated by

Leonard Swidler

REJECTION VERSUS REVELATION

Toward a Jewish Theology of Christianity

by

Lester Dean

I. INTRODUCTION

Jewish-Christian dialogue is now several decades old. In comparison to nearly two thousand years of dispute between the two religions, this is a very short period of time. In the past, Jews and Christians rejected each other's claim to a continuing, valid revelation from God. Jews who are engaged in dialogue with Christians are again confronted by the Christian claim to a revelation from God, but this claim is often made from a different perspective than in the past. The Christian partner in dialogue often affirms that neither Judaism nor Christianity comprehends the totality of God's truth, although both have received a revelation of that truth.[1] The goal of dialogue then is to "learn, change, and grow, not so we can force change on the other."[2]

How should Jews respond to this Christian claim within this new dialogical context? Is it possible for Jews to affirm that Judaism does not comprehend all divine truth, or at least not all of God's truth for all of humanity? Further, if Jews affirm the possibility that Christianity also has a revelation from God, will such an affirmation contract or endanger Judaism? Does an affirmation that Christianity has a divine revelation mean that Jews must also accept all Christian teachings and ultimately convert to Christianity?

Affirming that Judaism does not comprehend all divine truth is difficult for many Jews. The memories of past debates--not dialogues--which were usually instigated by Christian authorities to prove the superiority of Christianity and force Jews to convert, still linger. Such a past history often understandably produces the fear that if a Jew affirms that Judaism does not comprehend all divine truth the result would be conversion to Christianity. Thus the Jewish attitude is often that the Torah, as God's revelation to humanity, contains the totality of God's revelation. All that Jews need to comprehend God's truth is to study their own tradition. If God did reveal divine truth to non-Jews, such revelation should be considered inferior to the revelation of Torah and is of no interest to Jews.[3]

Such a viewpoint sees no value for Jews in inter-religious dialogue. However, although lingering fears may persist, the affirmation that Judaism does not comprehend all divine truth does not by necessity lead to conversion if such an affirmation is made within a dialogical context where the Christian partner makes a similar affirmation. In this case both have affirmed that neither religion comprehends all of God's truth for all of humanity. Neither will force change upon the other, and at least for some Christians dialogue has taken the place of a mission to the Jews.[4]

The removal of this fear of conversion is a necessary first step for Jews to participate in dialogue with Christians. However, it is not of itself a sufficient reason to affirm that Judaism does not contain all of God's revelation, nor does it automatically lead to the affirmation that Christianity does contain divine truth of value to the Jew. Such affirmations require a consideration of the process of receiving and interpreting God's revelation, which will now be discussed.

II. THE PROCESS OF REVELATION

Within Jewish tradition the prophet was the human vehicle for revelation. Revelation is often used to describe both the means by which God communicated with the prophet and the message which the prophet proclaimed.[5] In the Hebrew Scriptures there is little distinction between the means of revelation, the experience or realization of the divine word by the prophet, and the content of that revelation, the message or word of God spoken by the prophet. In most cases the prophet's role in the process was minimized. The prophet clearly comprehended God's message during the experience of revelation and proclaimed that message to the people, who were expected to hear, understand, and obey the divine message.

However, in the apocalyptic literature, including the book of Daniel, a distinction was made between the experience of revelation and the understanding of that message by the human recipient.[6] For example, Daniel received a vision from God, that is, he had a revelation experience. However, he did not understand that revelation until God, through the angel Gabriel, provided the interpretation of that vision, the message which he was to proclaim to the people.[7] Both the vision, as the experience, and the interpretation, the divine message to be proclaimed, were revelation from God, but they were two distinct events. The prophet's role was still passive; he was not as yet perceived as the interpreter of the divine message, but the distinction between revelatory experience and the message proclaimed provides the basis for considering the need to interpret divine revelation. The apocalyptic prophet was no longer the human mouthpiece repeating verbatim the divine communication he had experienced. The divine communication was itself unintelligible to the human recipient, and the prophet proclaimed not the original revelation but its interpretation.

Further thought about the process of revelation can be observed in the Qumran literature and in the rabbinic literature. For the Jews of the Qumran community the prophets of the Hebrew Scriptures proclaimed the revelation of God. However, the meaning of these revelations was unknown until God revealed their interpretation to the founder of the community, the Teacher of Righteousness.[8] In contrast to Daniel and the apocalyptic literature, the true meaning or content of the revelation was revealed to another peson at a much later time. Likewise, the rabbis concluded that "With the exception of Moses and Isaiah, none of the prophets knew the content of their prophecies."[9]

In this view of the revelation process both the reality of the experience of divine revelation and the need for interpreting that revelation by the later community were affirmed. Interpretation allowed the present community to make the revelation of others experienced in the past relevant to the present. Admittedly the present community took a dogmatic view about its interpretation of the revelation. There was only one true interpretation, that known to the community, and all others, whether in the past or yet to come in the future, were false. Yet the texts show that revelation was viewed as a more complex process. Both the prophet as proclaimer of the divine message, and the audience, as the hearers of that message, were now engaged in a process of interpreting God's word to humanity.

In the early years of the Common Era both Jews and Christians interpreted the Hebrew Scriptures and laid the foundations for Judaism and Christianity. Both affirmed that their own interpretations were revealed or inspired by God, faithfully presenting God's intended message inherent in the original revelation of the Bible, while the other's interpretations were false. For Judaism the original revelation of the Torah was supplemented by the oral law, which was collected in the Mishna and Gemora, and this body of literature, the Talmud, was the true interpretation of God's revelation. For Christianity the original revelation was supplemented by the teachings of Jesus and his apostles, which were collected in the New Testament, and this body of literature was the true interpretation of God's revelation.[10]

Nor did the process of interpretation cease with the Talmud and the New Testament. Both the synagogue and the church continued to reinterpret the revelation through the tradition of their respective communities. Thus it is an oversimplification to say that either of these religious traditions comprehends all of God's message for humanity. In one sense, because they have accepted a specific body of literature as the revelation of God, they have God's revelation in their possession. However, in another sense, because this literature must continually be interpreted within a living and changing community, neither comprehends all of God's message for humanity. It is possible that this continuing search for the interpretation of God's revelation can be enhanced through dialogue between Jews and Christians. However, dialogue requires more than just the realization that one's own tradition must continually be reinterpreted. It also requires the affirmation that the partner's tradition also contains God's revelation to humanity. For Jews to engage in dialogue with Christians they must also affirm that Christianity contains God's revelation for humanity and that this revelation has value for Jews as Jews. The problems that such an affirmation pose for Jews must now be considered.

III. THE IMPLICATIONS OF INTERPRETING REVELATION

The distinction previously made between God's revelation and the interpretation of the content of that revelation makes it possible for Jews to encounter the Christian claim that God gave humanity a revelation through Jesus without of necessity accepting the Christian interpretations of that revelation. However, what impetus is there for Jews to take seriously the Christian claim that their religion is based upon divine revelation? Why should Jews think that God used Jesus as a means of revelation, especially when the Christian interpretations of that revelation often seem to contradict the teachings of Judaism or even to deny the validity of Judaism?

The answer to this question is dependent upon one's view of history. From a Jewish viewpoint, and also from the viewpoint of most Christian traditions, history is not merely a product of human action but also the product of divine intervention. God, not humanity, is ultimately in control of history. This does not, of course, imply that all that happens in history is the product of divine will, but it does affirm the possibility that God can act in and through human history and that God's intervention in history has meaning and purpose. The experience of revelation, its interpretation, and its transmission all occur through God's action in human history. Conversely, it is possible that changes in history have special meaning and are to be considered revelations from God.[11]

Such a view of history as revelation is not without danger. History can only be viewed as revelation in retrospect, and revelation can conceivably be used to legitimize any event which occurred in history.[12] Thus it is important to have a standard with which to judge any claim that an event of history is a divine revelation. For Jews, this standard is the Hebrew Scriptures. The test of prophecy, and of all claims of revelation, must be compatibility with what Judaism has already accepted as revelation. For a historical event to be considered revelation for Jews, that event must not contradict Torah, and it must provide new information about God or humanity or the relationship between God and humanity.[13]

This was the criterion which Jewish tradition used in the past to evaluate the Christian claims of revelation. The Christian claim that Jesus was the messiah was considered contradictory to the role of the messiah found in Scripture. The Christian claim that Jesus was the Son of God was considered contradictory to the monotheism of Scripture. Thus these Christian interpretations were rejected, and Christianity was false.

The view of Saadia ha Gaon was typical: Christianity was a heresy.[14]

But a few Jewish writers, for example Judah ha Levi and Maimonides, also noted that Christianity converted many Gentiles from pagan idolatry.[15] This was seen as a first step in the conversion of the Gentiles to Judaism, which would occur in the messianic era. Even though most Christian teaching was in error, God still used the religion. Whatever divine truth Christianity affirmed had been derived from Judaism, not from divine revelation, but this divine truth did bring the world closer to God's goal for humanity. Such a view is far from an acceptance of Christianity, but, considering that for nearly two thousand years almost all Christians rejected Judaism and often persecuted Jews, such a view of Christianity by Jewish tradition should be praised for its positive character.

For most Jews there seems to be no reason to reconsider this traditional view of Christianity. Christianity is a mistake, but God has used the religion. Often Jews rely upon the Noahic laws to explain how Christians can be considered righteous even though Christianity is false.[16] Since the Noahic laws are often the basis for a Jewish evaluation of Christians, it is necessary to examine these laws to see if they contribute to a Jewish interpretation of Christianity.

IV. THE LAWS OF NOAH

The early rabbis were faced with the problem of affirming a universal God who created and cared for humanity, and at the same time affirmed that Judaism, their particular religion, was God's revealed message for humanity. If Jews were the chosen people of God, did this mean that all Gentiles were rejected by God unless they converted to Judaism? Such a view would surely contradict the affirmation that the God of the Jews was the single, loving, universal God of all humanity. Yet, if Gentiles were acceptable to God apart from Judaism, did this mean that Gentile religions were also God's revelation?

The response of the rabbis was that the righteous of all nations would participate in the world to come, and that anyone who did a good deed would be rewarded by God.[17] The criteria for righteous action was found through biblical exegesis. From Gen. 2:16 the rabbis deduced six laws which were given to Adam, and thus

86

known by all humanity and binding upon all humanity. There were five negative commandments prohibiting idolatry, blasphemy, murder, incest, and robbery; one positive commandment established courts of justice. These six commandments were repeated by God to Noah, along with the added prohibition of eating the flesh of live animals.[18] Other rabbis deduced up to thirty laws from Lev. 19:19 which they maintained Gentiles should obey.[19] It is unclear from the rabbinic material which laws has to be followed in order for Gentiles to be righteous, but by the time of Maimonides the righteous Gentile was the person who obeyed the seven laws of Noah.[20]

The question which should be considered is the value of using the Noahic laws today, within the context of interreligious dialogue. It is true that many Christians would agree that most, if not all, of these laws are God's commands and obey them.[21] However, Christians do not claim to be righteous merely by following these laws. They affirm that they have received a divine revelation through Jesus in which God established a covenant with them. The Noahic laws ignore the possibility of Christianity's being part of God's plan for humanity.

Jews have rejected the attempt by some Christians to explain the salvation of Jews through the principle of anonymous Christianity. According to this principle, Jews do not necessarily have to convert to Christianity in order to be righteous. Jews can follow Judaism and be righteous, but they are actually made righteous through Christ, not through Judaism, which has little, if any, value in God's plan for humanity.[22] Jews are righteous in spite of, and not because of, their Judaism.

The use of the Noahic laws by Jews is similar to the principle of anonymous Christianity and perhaps should be called anonymous Judaism. Christians do not need to convert to Judaism in order to be righteous. Christians can follow Christianity and be righteous, but they are actually made righteous through obedience to the Noahic laws, and not through Christianity, which has little, if any, value in God's plan for humanity. Christians are righteous in spite of, not because of, their Christianity.

Just as Jews have rejected the principle of anonymous Christianity, Christians have rejected the principle of the Noahic laws. Neither of these principles takes the other religion seriously. Neither is adequate for interreligious dialogue. If Jews want Christians to reconsider the validity of Judaism, then Jews must also reconsider the validity of Christianity. It is hypocrisy for Jews to demand that Christians accept the value of Judaism while they themselves use the Noahic laws to deny the value of Christianity.

Ultimately, it is faithfulness to God, the same God which Christians claim to worship, which is the impetus for a Jewish reconsideration of the Christian claim of receiving a revelation from God. Jewish tradition was confronted with the Christian interpretation of their revelation, rather than that revelation itself, and it was these interpretations that were rejected. If it is possible for Jews to distinguish between that Christian interpretation and the events which Christians claim to be revelation, then Jews should also examine those events to see whether they can be interpreted as a revelation from God. To refrain from such an attempt could mean that a revelation from God was being ignored because of the Christian interpretations of that revelation. Such an examination will not necessarily mean that Jews will change their views of Christianity or that they will accept Christian interpretations of the revelation claimed to have been received through Jesus. But it does mean that Jews will have taken seriously the possibility that God gave humanity a revelation through Jesus and will have judged for themselves whether revelation occurred.

But there is still one more problem which must be considered. The sources available for studying the events claimed by Christians to be revelation are themselves interpretations of that revelation. Is it possible, after nearly two thousand years, to distinguish between Christian interpretations and the events which may have been revelation? This is the question which will be discussed next.

V. THE SEARCH FOR THE HISTORICAL JESUS

A Jewish reconsideration of the possibility that God gave humanity a revelation through Jesus is faced with the problem that the sources which describe the events that might have been revelation are themselves Christian interpretations. New Testament scholars now recognize that the Gospels are not merely a biography of Jesus but are also theological statements about Jesus arising from the life situation of the early church. Form and redaction analysis attempt to rediscover the "historical Jesus," but there is still no consensus about the results of such inquiries.[23]

For the Jewish reader, the results of the above research are based upon questionable presuppositions. Although the purported goal of this research is the most accurate reconstruction of the life and teachings of Jesus, the Christian scholar often begins the inquiry within the theological presupposition that God did give the world a revelation through Jesus. Thus the focus is often upon the uniqueness of Jesus, whether as a person, or as a teacher, in order to provide a legitimation for Christianity. The Jewish reader does not share such presuppositions.

Prior to the nineteenth century the Jewish reader often started with a negative view of Jesus. This was the result of Christians' proclaiming their own Christian interpretations of Jesus to Jews. The rabbinic sources knew little about the life of Jesus. The rabbis rejected the Christian interpretations of Jesus and also the Jewishness of Jesus. Jesus was a magician or a heretic.[24] For Maimonides, Jesus was a false prophet who opposed Torah and rejected Judaism.[25] God gave no new revelation to humanity through Jesus, and both Jesus and Christianity were rejected.

Starting in the nineteenth century, Jews noted the distinction made by Christian scholars between Jesus and the Christian interpretations about Jesus. Jews turned to the Gospels along with Christian scholars in search of the "historical Jesus," and found that not only was Jesus born a Jew but also that the evidence showed he had not rejected Judaism. Jesus was seen as a typical Jew or sometimes as a prophet or even a great Jewish teacher.[26] For most of these Jewish authors Jesus either taught the same truths that Judaism had always taught, or else he had made various minor changes which were of no value to Judaism. Jesus was reclaimed by Jews, but no new revelation was found in his teachings.

This more positive view of Jesus the Jew was also accompanied by the separation of Jesus from Christianity. Many Christian scholars claimed that Christianity was either founded or radically altered by Paul, and Jewish writers accepted this view.[27] Any divine truth

Jesus proclaimed had already been a part of Judaism, and everything else in Christianity was a perversion of both the teachings of Jesus and of Judaism. Thus Christianity was a distorted form of Judaism for the Gentiles. The implication of such a view was still the same as that found in the earlier Jewish teachings about Christianity. If the errors in Christianity were removed, then the result would be Judaism, and Christians would necessarily convert to Judaism. The Jewish view of Jesus had changed, but not its view of Christianity.

A more positive view of Christianity was proposed by Franz Rosenzweig. Christianity had value in itself, not just as an intermediate step toward the conversion of the world to Judaism. For Rosenzweig, Christianity was the way of salvation for the Gentiles, and Jesus had a central, but theologically undefined role in God's salvation of the world.[28] Similar views have more recently been expressed by Pinchas Lapide and Will Herberg.[29] However, the exact role of Jesus in this plan has not as yet been formulated by these writers. They still find it difficult to determine how Jesus was used by God or to provide a Jewish interpretation for that revelation which Christians claim to have received through Jesus.

The search for the "historical Jesus" produced Jesus the Jewish teacher, but this Jesus seems inadequate as the foundation for Christianity. Yet this should not be surprising: Christianity is not based solely upon Jesus the Jew, but also upon Jesus the Christ of Christianity. Thus, in order to seek a Jewish interpretation of the Christian revelation through Jesus, it may be necessary to move from Jesus the Jewish teacher to Jesus the Christ of Christianity. However, such a change immediately becomes problematic for Jews. Is not one of the major differences between Judaism and Christianity the fact that Jews do not believe Jesus was the Christ, in contrast to Christians who do believe Jesus was, and is, the Christ? This problem requires a study of the role of human language in the interpretation of revelation, which will be discussed next.

VI. INTERPRETATION AND HUMAN LANGUAGE

The Christian belief that Jesus is the Christ is an interpretation of the revelation that they claim to have received through Jesus. Even in the Gospels, which, as noted in the previous section, are themselves Christian interpretations of the revelation of Jesus, the title of Christ is seldom attributed to Jesus. Only in the passion narrative of Mark 14 does Jesus grant that he is the Christ; but in the passion narratives of Matthew 26 and Luke 22 Jesus refuses to grant that he is the Christ. This particular Christian interpretation has been a problem for Jews, partly because of the problem of language.[30]

Both Jews and Christians share a common body of literature, the Hebrew Scriptures. Much of their language about their religious traditions has been derived from this common Scripture, leading to the assumption that there is a common religious language understandable to both Jews and Christians. However, both Judaism and Christianity also have a body of literature which is not shared by the other religious tradition, the Talmud and the New Testament. Because of this other literature, and because of a different history, Christian language is often not easily understood by Jews. The same words may be used, but with different meanings.

The Christian affirmation that Jesus is the Christ is an example of this problem of one word with different meanings in the two traditions. Christ is, of course, derived from christos, the Greek word for the Hebrew meshiach, or messiah, the anointed one. However, the word Christ as used by Christians is not merely a substitution of a Greek word for the Hebrew word messiah. The two words have very different meanings within Judaism and Christianity.

During the first centuries surrounding the Common Era there were several Jewish expectations about the role of the messiah. For some Jews the messiah would be an earthly ruler who would inherit the throne of David.[31] For other Jews the messiah would be a great general who would lead the Jews to victory over their enemies.[32] Still other Jews believed the messiah was a pre-existent heavenly figure who would come to earth to judge the world.[33]

The early followers of Jesus lived during this period of multiple definitions for the role of the messiah. They found it possible to use one or more of these definitions to interpret the revelation which they claimed to have received through Jesus. Thus for them Jesus was the messiah, and this message was

91

proclaimed both to their Jewish co-religionists and to interested Gentiles.

However, their message was not accepted by the majority of Jews. After the fall of the second temple, Judaism consolidated itself under the leadership of the rabbis at Yavneh. Out of this activity a single definition was accepted for the role of the messiah. The messiah was to be the agent of God causing or signaling the redemption of the physical world and reigning over the glorious age of peace and world prosperity.[34] According to this definition Jesus could not have been the messiah since the messianic kingdom on earth had not yet been established.

Thus the debate between Jews and Christians about whether Jesus was or was not the Christ is not about Jesus but about the correct definition for the role of the messiah or the Christ. Some Christians now engaged in dialogue with Jews have noted the difference between the definition for the role of the messiah in Judaism and in Christianity, and they support the right of Jews to define that role according to their own tradition. That is, they agree that according to the Jewish definition it is incorrect to claim that Jesus was the messiah.[35]

Likewise, the right to define the role of the messiah is not an exclusive Jewish right. Christians also have the right to their definition for the role of the messiah and proclaiming that according to that definition Jesus is the Christ. However, because of the difference in definitions, care must be taken by both traditions when using the term messiah or Christ.

It should also be noted that the Christian definition for messiah does not exclude the Jewish one, but broadens it. The Christian belief is that Jesus will also fulfill the Jewish definition at some future date, the "second coming." Some Jews today have noted that the possibility of Jesus' fulfilling the Jewish definition in the future cannot be absolutely rejected by Jews. Jewish tradition affirms that at least one great figure of the past, Elijah, will return when God's kingdom is established. If Elijah can return, it is not impossible that Jesus could likewise return. The difference between Jews and Christians, correctly noted by Pinchas Lapide, is that Christians, out of faith, proclaim that Jesus will return to fulfill the Jewish definition, while Jews, out of faith, proclaim that someone will come to fulfill that definition.[36] It is possible that it could be Jesus, but it is the coming of the messiah, and not the identity of the messiah, that is of most importance to Jews.

The reason for the Jewish denial that Jesus was the Christ according to a Jewish definition is now understandable. However, a Jewish reaction to the Christian view of Jesus as the Christ according to the Christian definition has not yet been discussed, for several reasons. First, there is no single Christian definition for the role of Christ, not even a single definition within the New Testament.[37] The numerous meanings for the Christian affirmation that Jesus is the Christ can be noted in any volume on Christology. To address even a representative selection in this discusssion would be impossible.

Second, each of the definitions raises the same problem of language which was found previously. What does the Christian mean by affirming that Jesus is the Christ, and defining Christ to mean, for example, the Son of God or the Savior of the world? The meanings of each of these definitions are themselves unclear, and a definition for Christ which might at first appear to be contradictory to Judaism could actually be caused by the language used. For example, most Jews believe that to claim Jesus is the Son of God is contradictory to Judaism, yet some Christian explanations of the meaning of Son of God are not contradictory to Jewish mono-theistic beliefs.[38]

Finally, evaluating the various Christian claims about Jesus is only evaluating Christian definitions of the revelation which they claimed to have received through Jesus. Even if it were possible to examine each of these interpretations, and even if each were found to be contradictory to Judaism, the role of Jesus for Jews would not have been answered. All that would have been accomplished would be a comprehensive Jewish critique of Christianity, which is not the purpose of this discussion. Rather, the question which has been posed is whether it is possible to find a Jewish inter-pretation of Jesus as God's revelation.[39] In order to accomplish this goal, the events which led Christians to affirm that they received a revelation through Jesus must be examined--the crucifixion, resurrection and ascension of Jesus.

VII. THE DEATH OF JESUS

Within Jewish tradition revelation is usually associated with the prophets and their proclamations to the people. However, the prophets related the revelation of God not only through prophetic oracles, but also through their actions and lives. Moses and Aaron performed specific acts, revealing to both the Israelites and the Egyptians the God of Abraham through the working of signs and wonders. Samuel used the tearing of Saul's robe to show that he had lost the kingdom. Jeremiah wore the iron yoke of Babylon; Ezekiel enacted the siege of Jerusalem; and Hosea showed God's love for Israel by his marriage to the harlot Gomer. Thus the revelation of a prophet included, but was not limited to, the words of the prophet. The life of the prophet could also be used as a revelation from God.

In a similar manner, the possibility that God gave humanity a revelation through Jesus should not be limited to the teachings of Jesus. The view of Jesus as the great Jewish teacher was discussed earlier. Limiting attention to only the teachings of Jesus does remind both Jews and Christians that Jesus was a Jew. However, no new revelation from God was found in these teachings. Jesus the Jew has nothing to teach Judaism and provides no theological explanation for Christianity.

Nor does Christianity limit its focus only to the teachings of Jesus. The revelation of God through Jesus included the crucifixion of Jesus and the Christian belief that Jesus was resurrected and ascended into heaven. These were the events which formed the core of the new revelation from God, and which became the foundation for Christianity.[40] How are Jews to respond to the Christian claim that these events were revelations from God?

Both Jews and Christians have accepted the historicity of the crucifixion of Jesus but have disagreed about its being a new revelation from God. Christians have usually explained the meaning of the crucifixion as a sacrifice by which God saved humanity. The concept that people can benefit from the suffering of the innocent can be found in Jewish tradition.[41] Human experience itself shows that the suffering of the righteous can influence the lives of others. This is only too painfully apparent to Jews after the

94

Holocaust. The lives of both Jews and Christians have been changed because of the suffering and death of these innocent victims.

However, the question which Jews ask Christians is exactly how the death of Jesus was unique. It is possible that Jesus was a righteous person whose death was used by God in a special way to save humanity, but such an explanation for the death of Jesus can never be verified through history. It depends solely upon belief in Christian doctrine, as an attempt to find transcendent meaning for the death of Jesus. Judaism affirms that a person can benefit from the sufferings of others but not that a person must benefit from the suffering of another. An exclusive Christian claim that a person can obtain righteousness only through the death of Jesus contradicts the fundamental Jewish belief that righteousness is obtained through the Mosaic covenant.

From a Jewish viewpoint meaning can be found in the death of Jesus, but this meaning is not a new revelation from God. The crucifixion of Jesus reaffirms what Judaism knew from its own Scripture and history, that a human being can yield one's self totally to God's will and become a martyr for God and humanity. Such a Jewish interpretation for the crucifixion of Jesus may seem inadequate to Christians since it does not claim uniqueness for Jesus. Others have revealed a similar love for God and humanity. Yet this does not lessen the value of such a sacrifice. As John 15:13 states, "No one has greater love than the person who is voluntarily killed for one's friends" (translation mine). From this viewpoint both Jews and Christians can agree that Jesus again revealed the great truth that human beings can sacrifice themselves for God and humanity.

However, the above meaning for the death of Jesus still provides no foundation for Christianity from a Jewish viewpoint, since the meaning for the death of Jesus is not a new revelation from God. According to Christianity, the crucifixion of Jesus was not the end. Rather, it was the prelude to other events, the resurrection and ascension of Jesus. Without a belief in these events it is doubtful if Christianity would exist. To ignore them is to ignore part of the core of Christianity; yet most Jews believe that to accept them is to cross the line between Judaism and Christianity.

Thus it is the possibility of the resurrection of Jesus which now must be studied.

VIII. THE POSSIBILITY OF JESUS' RESURRECTION

The resurrection of Jesus is viewed by most Christians as a revelation from God. There has been great disagreement in the past between Jews and Christians about the resurrection.[42] Jews have traditionally denied the historicity of the resurrection, and thus denied the possibility that it was a revelation from God. However, the reason for this rejection was probably due to the Christian interpretations of the resurrection of Jesus. These Christian interpretations should not be used as the grounds for a Jewish denial for the possibility of the resurrection of Jesus. Rather, the possibility of the resurrection must be judged by the criteria of Jewish tradition.

In recent years both Herschel Matt and Pinchas Lapide have observed that Jews need not deny the possibility of the resurrection of Jesus.[43] The Hebrew Scriptures and post-biblical literature speak of God's raising or reviving the dead, in some cases referring to a resuscitated corpse, and in others referring to a messianic resurrection of the dead.[44] The rabbinic tradition derived its belief in the future messianic resurrection from various biblical texts and stated that those who denied the resurrection would have no place in the world to come.[45] The hope for the future resurrection was even included in the Jewish liturgy as the second benediction of the Amida, "Blessed art thou, O LORD, who revivest the dead."

Thus there is nothing in Jewish tradition which requires a Jew to deny the possibility that God raised Jesus from the dead, nor does the acceptance of the resurrection of Jesus necessitate a conversion from Judaism to Christianity. It is not the possibility of the resurrection that is a problem, but its possible meaning.

Both Matt and Lapide argue that Jews should find no religious meaning in the possible resurrection of Jesus.[46] However, such a position does not seem to take seriously the possibility of the resurrection of Jesus. If Jesus was resurrected by God, then it was an instance of divine intervention into human history. Christian Scripture affirms that God raised Jesus from the dead; it was not the act of Jesus alone.[47] If

96

there was such an extraordinary intervention of God into human history, then this must have been done for some reason. To acknowledge the possibility of the resurrection, but deny that it has any meaning, is to affirm that God's acts in history are capricious and without meaning. Such a view is surely contrary to Judaism, which affirms that God's action in history is significant and should be understood as revelation.

Jewish reluctance to find a religious meaning in the possible resurrection of Jesus is probably due to the fear that acceptance of such a meaning will necessitate an acceptance of Christian beliefs about Jesus and a denial of Judaism. A religious meaning for the possible resurrection of Jesus does not mean that a Jew must accept a role for Jesus beyond that of a Jewish teacher or prophet. Jewish tradition affirms that God's intervention into history on behalf of a person or on behalf of a people does not demonstrate that that person or people is in any way superior to others. God chose the Jews as a people not because they were superior to others but, rather, out of love for Israel and humanity.[48] Likewise the prophets of Israel often affirmed their own unworthiness.[49] By analogy, the possibility of God's resurrection of Jesus is a sign of God's love and not necessarily a sign that Jesus was a special person. If there is a religious meaning for the possible resurrection of Jesus, it should involve a message from God to humanity, and not a verification of a special identity or role for Jesus.

Nor is this view of the interpretation of the resurrection contradictory to the New Testament. The Christian Scriptures do not clearly state that the resurrection of Jesus proved that he was the messiah or the Son of God. Rather, Jesus was resurrected so that he could be the savior or the judge of the world.[50] The emphasis is upon the resurrection as part of God's plan for the salvation of humanity. It showed God's love for humanity, and allowed Christians to affirm in faith that Jesus would return as savior and judge. It seems that the emphasis upon the resurrection as proof of the special identity of Jesus was a later Christian interpretation.

Thus it is not only possible for Jews to believe in the resurrection of Jesus, but this resurrection should also be considered meaningful, as part of a message from God to humanity. The question then is what that meaning might be within a Jewish context, and whether that meaning necessitates a Jewish affirmation that Jesus was resurrected by God.

IX. THE RESURRECTION, ASCENSION AND GENTILE MISSION

In order to suggest a Jewish interpretation for the possible resurrection of Jesus, it is necessary to examine the changes brought about by the early Christians who viewed that event as revelation, rather than the Christian interpretations of that event. That is, how was human history changed because of the Christian belief that Jesus was resurrected?

Such a study is difficult because the sources themselves are theological and not just historical documents. The minimum which can be said with assurance is that a fearful group who had been followers of Jesus were briefly reunited with their crucified leader. Some of them believed Jesus would immediately establish the messianic kingdom, but instead of establishing this kingdom Jesus ascended into heaven. Shortly thereafter these followers of Jesus had such an intense religious experience that they were compelled to proclaim to both their fellow Jews and to interested Gentiles that Jesus had been raised from the dead and would return shortly to judge the world. To the Gentiles they added the message that conversion to Judaism was not a necessity to enter into the kingdom of God.[51]

The message that God would establish a messianic kingdom and that this kingdom would soon become a reality was not an addition to Jewish teaching; it was a common theme in all apocalyptic Jewish literature. Although the impetus for such a proclamation by the early Christians may have been the resurrection of Jesus, this proclamation cannot be viewed as a new revelation from God.

However, the impetus for an active mission to the Gentiles in which they were converted from paganism, but not to Judaism, could be viewed as a new revelation. According to the Gospels Jesus spoke almost exclusively to Jews and was involved only reluctantly with Gentiles.[52] It was only after the resurrection that Jesus was understood to have commanded his followers to preach to Gentiles.[53] Likewise, the earliest preaching of the disciples was to Jews, and divine guidance was given to Peter and Paul to preach to the Gentiles.[54] Thus it appears that the early

98

Christians saw the mission to the Gentiles as a new revelation from God, connected with the resurrection of Jesus.

The New Testament does not provide the details about how the resurrection of Jesus revealed the need for a mission to the Gentiles. The following is one possible way to connect the resurrection with that mission, and thus one possible interpretation for the message of the revelation which can be found in the resurrection of Jesus. It is not presented as proven history, or as the only interpretation for the resurrection of Jesus.

The followers of Jesus expected the messianic kingdom to be established immediately after the resurrection of Jesus.[55] But with the ascension of Jesus its establishment was postponed. God could have established the kingdom but apparently had decided not to do so. The reason for this postponement was to allow time for the Gentiles to convert from paganism and thus become part of the future kingdom. That is, God delayed the kingdom out of love for the Gentiles.[56]

The resurrection and ascension of Jesus enabled God to show divine love for the Gentiles in a new way. Judaism had proclaimed God's love for humanity, but this love was in some sense secondary to God's love for Israel. The Jews had been chosen by God in a special way, by the establishment of the covenant with God at Sinai and the receiving of the Torah. The messianic kingdom was primarily a benefit for the Jews, God's chosen people, then secondarily a benefit for Gentiles. The Jewish message to the Gentiles was that God loved humanity, and that this love had been shown by God's choice of the Jews.

The message of the early Christians did not deny this Jewish message, but added to it. God loved the Jews, and they did in some sense occupy a special place in God's plan for humanity.[57] But the postponement of the kingdom showed to the Gentiles the great extent of God's love for them. God delayed the benefits of the kingdom intended for the Jews so that the Gentiles could also participate in the kingdom.

Clearly, such a message was a new expression of God's love for the Gentiles, but was it also a new revelation to the Jews? That is, did the Jews at this time believe that the Gentiles should be converted from paganism before the establishment of the kingdom?

There is evidence of proselytism by Jews at this time, so a mission to Gentiles would not have been contrary to Jewish teaching.[58] However, there is little evidence that the Jews believed that most Gentiles would be converted before the establishment of the messianic kingdom. The Hebrew Scriptures were vague about the exact time when the Gentiles would be converted from paganism.[59] In almost all of the post-biblical literature in which the worship of God by the Gentiles was mentioned, this worship took place after the messianic kingdom had been established.[60] Therefore, the Christian message that the Gentiles would be converted before the messianic kingdom was established can be viewed as a new revelation to the Jews. This revelation did not contradict the Hebrew Scriptures but explained in greater detail the revelation contained in that Scripture.

Based upon the above discussion, one Jewish interpretation of the possible resurrection and ascension of Jesus could be that it revealed to both Jews and Gentiles that God loved all humanity and that all the world should worship God before the establishment of the messianic kingdom. Such an interpretation makes the affirmation of Christians, that they have experienced God's love through Jesus, understandable for Jews. God showed divine love for the Gentiles by revealing through the resurrection and ascension of Jesus that the establishment of the messianic kingdom would be delayed so that the Gentiles could also become part of the people of God.

X. REVELATION AND GENTILE CONVERSION TO JUDAISM

The early Christians, and especially Paul, found a second revelation from God through Jesus that was relevant to the Gentiles. Not only was there to be a mission to the Gentiles, but the Gentiles did not, and should not, become Jews in order to become part of the people of God. Gentiles were able to worship God without accepting all the commandments of Torah.

There is evidence for interpreting this as a second new revelation from God. In the Hebrew Scriptures and the post-biblical literature, Gentile religions were considered idolatrous, and Gentiles were righteous only when they worshipped God.[61] Thus the

100

Gentiles should convert from paganism to the worship of God. Both Jews and the early Christians were in agreement about the desirability of this Gentile conversion.

However, the question which was not clearly answered in the Hebrew Scriptures was whether this worship of God by Gentiles meant that the Gentiles had to convert to Judaism and follow Torah. In some of the post-biblical and rabbinic literature the Gentiles were condemned not only for idolatry but also for not following Torah.[62] These texts imply that Gentiles must convert to Judaism in order to be righteous. As noted earlier, there are also rabbinic texts which affirm that Gentiles did not have to convert to Judaism in order to be righteous, but it is questionable whether this second view can be dated to the time of Jesus. It is probable that the early Christians proclaimed the message that Gentiles did not have to convert to Judaism before such a view had been accepted within Judaism, especially since the issue was debated within the early Christian community.[63]

The connection between Jesus and this new revelation that Gentiles should not convert to Judaism has yet to be clearly defined. Part of the problem is that in the past Christian scholars interpreted Paul to be contrasting faith in Jesus with Jewish legalism. It was believed that Judaism affirmed that one was made righteous by keeping the commandments of Torah, and that Paul was arguing for reliance upon the grace of God, instead of upon human works. Thus Judaism was obsolete both for Jews and for Gentiles, and there was no reason to inquire why the early Christians proclaimed that Gentiles should not follow Torah; no one should follow Torah.

Some Christian scholars now realize that Judaism was not a legalistic religion. A person was not made righteous by following Torah, but by God's gracious act of establishing the covenant. Following Torah was the correct response of the person who was righteous, and not following Torah caused the righteous person to become unrighteous. Thus the contrast between Jewish legalism and Christian faith is incorrect. Paul addressed Gentiles and proclaimed that they should not follow Torah, but he did not proclaim that Jews should not follow Torah.[64]

The research about how Paul came to the realization that Gentiles should not convert to Judaism is just beginning, and thus the connection between Jesus and his message is still unclear. Paul's message to the Gentiles was not based upon the belief that it was impossible to follow Torah, for he affirmed that he followed it blamelessly: Phil. 3:6. Perhaps a clue can be found in Gal. 5:2-6, where Paul stated both that Christ was of no advantage to the Gentile who became a Jew and also that it makes no difference whether a person is a Jew or a Gentile. The emphasis is upon how a Gentile, who is now a Christian, will have righteousness. If law, nomos, refers primarily to the Jewish cult in these passages, and not to following Torah, Paul's statements would be in harmony with Jewish beliefs at the time. The contrast Paul was making would then be between the sacrificial death of Jesus as the Christ and the Jewish sacrificial cult. The Gentile remains righteous because of Christ's death and does not need to be involved with Jewish sacrifices. However, if the Gentile converts to Judaism, then he or she must participate in the cult and the death of Christ is of no value. Although only a tentative suggestion, this would link the new revelation that Gentiles should not convert to Judaism with the death of Jesus.[65]

XI. THE REVELATION THROUGH JESUS AND JUDAISM TODAY

The interpretations suggested above for God's revelation through Jesus are dependent upon accepting the resurrection and Christian, not Jewish, beliefs. The interpretations do not contradict Judaism and thus can be accepted by Jews without requiring conversion to Christianity. However, one further question must be considered. Is it necessary for the Jews to accept the resurrection and ascension?

The interpretations for the possible resurrection and ascension of Jesus were shown to be new revelations to the Jews of the time of Jesus. However, in the centuries since the beginning of the Common Era the messages found in these interpretations have become part of Judaism. Although an active mission to the Gentiles is not a part of all Jewish movements, the belief that Gentiles will participate in the messianic kingdom--and that conversion to Judaism is not a prerequisite for such participation--is part of basic Jewish teaching. Jews need not affirm the resurrection and ascension of Jesus in order to affirm these truths. Thus there is no necessity for Jews to accept the resurrection or ascension of Jesus.

However, the interpretations suggested for the resurrection and ascension of Jesus are options for Jews. These interpretations make it possible for Jews to affirm the resurrection and ascension of Jesus while remaining true to Judaism. Further, these interpretations provide a theological foundation for Jews to acknowledge the validity of Christianity. God could have used Jesus as a means of giving humanity new revelation. Thus Christianity can be viewed as part of God's plan for humanity. This does not mean that Jews totally agree with all Christian teachings, but it does provide one way to affirm that Christians as Christians, rather than as righteous Gentiles, are part of the people of God.

XII.   CONCLUSION

The above is one Jewish interpretation of the possible resurrection and ascension of Jesus as a revelation from God. It attempts to take seriously the Christian affirmations about Jesus and to interpret these from a Jewish viewpoint. It is a Jewish interpretation of these events, not a Jewish critique of Christian interpretations. Meanings were found for the resurrection and ascension of Jesus which do not contradict Jewish teaching and which can be viewed as revelation from God. I ask other Jews and Christians interested in dialogue both to critique this attempt seriously, and to offer interpretations of their own so that there can be a mutual understanding of God's truth for humanity.

Through his life and death Jesus showed God's love for humanity, the need for humans to love God, and the need for humans to love one another. Both Jews and Christians can affirm that the two great commandments to love God and to love one's neighbor are found in the Torah and the Gospels.

God also used Jesus to show divine love for humanity and, in particular, love for the Gentiles. Jews have experienced God's love through their own tradition, especially through their special covenant with God at Sinai. However, to a certain extent, this love requires the existence of non-Jews. God's love for the Jews is connected with their election as God's people. Without the existence of non-Jews, the experiencing of this love of God by the Jews could be obscured. Would not the concept of election change if there were only Jews in the world?

Emphasis by Jews upon Jewish election can also lead to a subordination of God's love for all humanity. God can become primarily the Jewish God, and only secondarily the God of all the world. The suggested interpretation of the possible resurrection of Jesus can remind Jews that God is the God of all and loves all of humanity.

In a similar manner, Christians experience God's love for humanity through Jesus. The resurrection of Jesus and the delay of the messianic kingdom showed God's great love for the non-Jews. This love experienced by the Gentiles also requires, to a certain extent, the existence of the Jews. To restate the Christian expression of God's love found in John 3:16 from a Jewish perspective: God so loved the world that God delayed establishing the messianic kingdom after the resurrection of Jesus so that Gentiles could turn to God and participate in that kingdom. Without the existence of the Jews, the experiencing of this love of God by the Gentiles could be obscured. Would not the concept of equal participation in the messianic kingdom change if there were only Gentiles in the world?

Emphasis by Christians upon God's love for them as revealed by the resurrection of Jesus can also lead to a subordination of God's love for the Jews. God can become primarily the Christian God, and Jews can be accused of rejecting that God because they are not Christians. From a historical viewpoint the Christian neglect of God's continuing love for the Jews has had disastrous consequences, leading to Jewish oppression and death. The suggested interpretation of the possible resurrection of Jesus can remind Christians that God is also the God of the Jews.

Thus the suggested interpretation for the revelation of Jesus affirms God's love for both Jews and Christians. This divine love is most apparent because of the existence of both Jews and Christians. The interpretation of the revelation can be used by either Jews or Christians to guard against their claiming exclusive possession of God's love.

Both Judaism and Christianity have used biblical stories about brothers to illustrate the relationship of the two traditions to God and to each other. Jews used the relationship between Jacob and Esau. The Jews, symbolized by Jacob, valued God's commandments, while the Christians, symbolized by Esau, placed no

104

value upon God's commandments and were glad to exchange them for something of lesser value, as Esau did when he sold his birthright. Thus the Jews were the chosen of God, while the Christians rejected God.

Christianity used the story of Ishmael and Isaac to symbolize the relationship between Judaism and Christianity. The Jews, symbolized by Ishmael, were the children of Hagar, the slave, who tried to please God by vain deeds rather than by faith. They were not the true children of God. The Christians, symbolized by Isaac, were the children of Sarah, the children of promise, who pleased God through faith. They were the true children of God who had replaced the Jews.

After two thousand years of sibling rivalry, it is time to replace these two stories with one which can affirm the mutual validity of Judaism and Christianity and their interdependence in the service of God. An appropriate story to symbolize such a relationship would be that of Moses and Aaron. Moses was the recipient of God's revelation, but Aaron was needed to help relate the message of that revelation to the people. Both brothers were necessary for God's plan for humanity, and they worked together to bring about God's plan of redemption.

Both Jews and Christians, like Moses, claim to have received a revelation from God for humanity. Both Jews and Christians, like Aaron, can help explain the revelation of the other to all of humanity. Jews and Christians can fulfill both roles, especially through dialogue. They can proclaim their own message and help to interpret the message of the other, not as rivals, but as siblings, workers together helping to bring about the common hope of both traditions, the creation of God's kindgom of righteousness, equality and peace on earth.

1 For examples of this position see John Hick, God Has Many Names (Philadelphia: Westminster, 1982), pp. 48-54, 91-94, 110-115, 124-127; Donald Swearer, Dialogue, the Key to Understanding Other Religions (Philadelphia: Westminster, 1977), pp. 33-35, 46-48; Leonard Swidler, "The Dialogue Decalogue: Ground Rules for Interreligious Dialogue," Journal of Ecumenical Studies, vol. 20 (1983), p. 4.

2 Swidler, "Dialogue Decalogue," p. 2.

3 For a characteristic argument against dialogue see Eliezer Berkovits, "Judaism in the Post-Christian Era," Judaism, vol. 15 (1966), pp. 79-82. For arguments in favor of dialogue see Walter Jacobs, Christianity through Jewish Eyes (Cincinnati: HUC, 1974), pp. 237-238; Henry Siegman, "Dialogue with Christians: A Jewish Dilemma," Judaism, vol. 20 (1971), p. 94; Abraham Heschel, "No Religion Is an Island," in F. E. Talmage, ed., Disputation and Dialogue (New York: KTAV, 1975), pp. 345-346. For one Jewish argument for viewing other religions as equal revelations from God see Dan Cohn-Sherbok, "Judaism and the Universe of Faith," New Blackfriars, vol. 65 (1984), pp. 28-35.

4 For examples for this view on missions see Markus Barth, Israel and the Church (Richmond: Knox, 1969), p. 16; A. Roy Eckardt, Elder and Younger Brothers (New York: Shocken, 1967), p. 152; Krister Stendahl, Paul among Jews and Gentiles (Philadelphia: Fortress, 1976), p. 4.

5 Revelation has been defined by some Jewish writers as divine self-disclosure, and not as a message for humanity, e.g., Franz Rosenzweig, Franz Rosenzweig, His Life and Thought, Nahum Glatzer, ed. (New York: Shocken, 1961), p. 285; Louis Jacob, A Jewish Theology (New York: Behrman, 1973), pp. 203-210. A contrary definition, similar to the one adopted in this discussion, can be found in Abraham Heschel, God in Search of Man (New York: Farrar, Strauss, Cudahy, 1955), p. 261. Defining revelation as God's message for humanity is not meant to refute the view that an individual does, in some sense, experience God's self-disclosure in revelation. However, Jewish tradition has, in general, been more concerned with the content of the revelation,

i.e., the message God has communicated. Revelation as divine self-disclosure raises the questions of the extent to which any human being can comprehend God, and how the experience of revelation can be communicated to another individual. Revelation as message presupposes that human beings can and are intended to understand the contents of revelation. The definition of revelation as a divine self-disclosure may be useful in Jewish-Christian dialogue concerning the relationship of Jesus and God and the meaning of the Christian claim that Jesus is the Son of God. E.g., see the discussion of Christian trinitarian beliefs by Paul van Buren, Discerning the Way (New York: Seabury, 1980), pp. 78-86. Revelation is not defined as divine self-disclosure by van Buren, yet a Jewish definition of revelation as divine self-disclosure could be an appropriate starting point for evaluating his definition of Jesus as Son of God.

[6] The term "post-biblical literature" is used to denote such Jewish writings as the Apocrypha, Pseudepigrapha, the Qumran Scrolls and the writings of Josephus and Philo. It essentially covers that body of Jewish literature which is part of neither the Hebrew Scripture nor the rabbinic literature. In Christian terminology this literature is often called the "intertestamental literature."

[7] Dan. 8-9. For examples from apocalyptic literature see Ap. Ab. 9-12, 20-21; 2 Bar. 35-36, 53-54; 4 Ezra 11-13.

[8] 1QpH 2:8-10, 7:1-5; CD 1:12-13; 1QS 11:5-8.

[9] Mid. Ps. 90:1; Yalkit 2:368; Eccl. Rab. 1:8; Lev. Rab. 1:14; Philo, Special Laws, 1:63.

[10] Jewish tradition has maintained an uneasy balance between the view that all revelation and its interpretation was given to Moses at Sinai, including the oral tradition found in the Talmud, and the need for continuing interpretation of revelation. Scripture had several interpretations, San. 34a, and Moses was not aware of all these future interpretations, San. 22a. Further, some of what had been revealed to Moses had been forgotten and had to be derived from the Torah, Tem. 16a, Men. 29b. Thus there was a need for continued interpretation, and detailed rules for this interpretation were established, Tos. San. 7:11; Sif. 1c. See also Emil Fackenheim, Quest for Past and

Future (Bloomington: Indiana University Press, 1968), pp. 80-81, 107-108, 307-308; H. Loewe in C. Montefiore and H. Loewe, eds., A Rabbinic Anthology (Philadelphia: Jewish Publication Society, 1951), lxiv-lxxi; Heschel, God in Search of Man, pp. 264-266.

11 For a Jewish discussion of history as revelation see Heschel, God in Search of Man, pp. 200-206; Montefiore and Loewe, A Rabbinic Anthology, p. xxiii; Fackenheim, Quest for Past and Future, p. 79; Arthur Cohen, Natural and Supernatural Jew (London: Valentine, Mitchell, 1967), p. 302; Will Herberg, Judaism and Modern Man (Philadelphia: JPS, 1951), pp. 194-195, 219, 226, 247-250). For a similar Christian view see van Buren, Discerning the Way, pp. 166-183.

12 See Herberg, Judaism and Modern Man, pp. 197-198; Fackenheim, Quest for Past and Future, p. 109.

13 The criteria for prophecy is found in Deut. 13:1-5. Even miracles and a voice from heaven were subordinate to human interpretation of Torah, Ba Mez 59b. Jewish tradition did affirm that prophecy ceased with the prophet Malachi, but this end of prophecy should not be interpreted as the end of revelation; see Tos. Sot. 132; Heschel, God in Search of Man, p. 255; Cohen, Natural and Supernatural Jew, p. 305.

14 J. Heineman, Three Jewish Philosophers (Philadelphia: Jewish Publication Society, 1960), p. 103. For similar views from modern Jews see Berkovits, "Judaism in the Post-Christian Era," p. 80; Jacob Taubes, "The Issues between Judaism and Christianity," in A. Cohen, ed., Arguments and Doctrines (New York: Harper and Row, 1970), p. 408; Arthur Cohen, The Myth of the Judaeo-Christian Tradition (New York: Schocken, 1971), p. 40.

15 Heineman, Three Jewish Philosophers, p. 121; Maimonides, Mishnah Torah Hil Mel 11, vol. 14. For similar modern views see Lowell Streiker, "The Modern Jewish-Christian Dialogue," Journal of Ecumenical Studies, vol. 2 (1965), p. 110.

16 See Eugene Borowitz, "A Jewish Response," in D. Dawe and J. Carman, eds., Christian Faith in a Religiously Plural World (Maryknoll: Orbis, 1978), p. 61.

[17] Kid. 40a; Meg. 13a; San. 59a; Ab. Zara. 3a; Tos. San. 13:2. See also Montefiore and Loewe, A Rabbinic Anthology, pp. 556-558.

[18] San. 56 a, b.

[19] Hullin 92a.

[20] Maimonides, Mishnah Torah Hil Mell 11, vol. 14.

[21] The definition of idolatry and whether Christians were idolators were debated by the rabbis and medieval commentators. The majority view was that Christians were not idolators, San. 56a, b, 63a; Hullin 13b; Meg. 28a; Bek. 2b. See also Pinchas Lapide, Israelis, Jews and Jesus (Garden City: Doubleday, 1979), p. 85; Raphael Loewe, Studies in Rationalism, Judaism, and Universalism (New York: Humanities Press, 1966), p. 138; Bernard Drachman, "Jewish-Gentile Relations Considered from the Jewish Viewpoint," in L. Jung, ed., Judaism in a Changing World, vol. 4 (London and New York: Soncino Press, 1971), pp. 120-121.

[22] See Barth, Israel and the Church, p. 36; Paul Knitter, No Other Name (Maryknoll: Orbis, 1985), pp. 120-141.

[23] For a discussion of the search for the historical Jesus see Martin Kähler, The So-called Historical Jesus and the Historic Christ (Philadelphia: Fortress, 1964); J. M. Robinson, A New Quest for the Historical Jesus (Naperville: Allenson, 1959); Heinz Zahrnt, The Historical Jesus (New York: Harper & Row, 1963); Norman Perrin, Rediscovering the Teaching of Jesus (New York: Harper & Row, 1967).

[24] San. 43a, 107b; Sot. 47b; Ab. Zara. 1b, 17a. See also Joseph Klausner, Jesus of Nazareth (New York: Macmillan, 1953), pp. 18-47.

[25] I. Twersky, A Maimonides Reader (New York: Berhman, 1972), pp. 441-447.

[26] For summaries of Jewish views about Jesus see Shalom Ben-Chorin, "The Image of Jesus in Modern Judaism," Journal of Ecumenical Studies, vol. 11 (1974), pp. 408-441; Lapide, Israelis, Jews and Jesus, pp. 106-128; and Günther Baumbach, "Fragen der modernen jüdische Jesusforschung an die christliche Theologie,"

Theologische Literaturzeitung, vol. 9 (1977), pp. 626-635.

[27] For Jews with this view see Lapide, *Israelis, Jews, and Jesus*, pp. 110, 134; Klausner, *Jesus of Nazareth*, pp. 370, 390; Samuel Sandmel, *The Genius of Paul* (New York: Farrar, Straus, Cudahy, 1958), p. 211.

[28] Glatzer, *Franz Rosenzweig, His Life and Thought*, pp. 27, 341-342.

[29] Will Herberg, *Faith Enacted as History* (Philadelphia: Westminster, 1976), pp. 29, 86; Pinchas Lapide and Jürgen Moltmann, *Jewish Monotheism and Christian Trinitarian Doctrine*, tr. Leonard Swidler (Philadelphia: Fortress, 1981), pp. 59, 69, 76.

[30] For a discussion of the role of language in interreligious dialogue see Raimundo Pannikar, *The Intra-religious Dialogue* (New York: Paulist, 1978), pp. xxv-xxvi; Wilfred Cantwell Smith, *Towards a World Theology* (Philadelphia: Westminster, 1981), pp. 60, 97.

[31] 4QD; 4 Ezra 7; 2 Bar. 27-30; Ps. Sol. 17-18.

[32] 1QM 5:1, 12:10-15; 1QSb 5:21-28; 4 Ezra 12-13; 2 Bar. 39-40, 69-74.

[33] 4Q243, 1 En. 7:26-30, 12:32, 14:9; 2 Bar. 30:1.

[34] San. 98b; Ket. 111b; Sif. Deut. 32:13; Num. Rab. 13:2, 14; Pes. Rab. 162 a, b. However, this Jewish definition for the messianic role developed over a period of time; see Abba Hillel Silver, *A History of Messianic Speculation in Israel* (Boston: Beacon Press, 1959), pp. 13-30.

[35] E.g., see Eckardt, *Elder and Younger Brothers*, pp. 131, 135, 143; Rosemary Ruether, *Faith and Fratricide* (New York: Seabury, 1979), p. 245; Leonard Swidler, "The Jewishness of Jesus," *Journal of Ecumenical Studies*, vol. 18 (1981), pp. 109, 113.

[36] Lapide, *Jewish Monotheism and Christian Trinitarian Doctrine*, p. 79. See also David Flusser, "To What Extent Is Jesus a Question for the Jews?" in Hans Küng and Walter Kasper, eds., *Christians and Jews* (New York: Seabury, 1974), pp. 70-71.

[37] For an introduction to the problem see Eva Fleischner, Judaism in Genuine Christian Theology (Metuchen, NJ: Scarecrow, 1975), p. 135.

[38] E.g., see Monica Hellwig, "The Christ of Dogma," in Alan Davies, ed., Anti-Semitism and the Foundations of Christianity (New York: Paulist, 1979), p. 124; Barth, Israel and the Church, p. 19; van Buren, Discerning the Way, pp. 85-89.

[39] This is an important distinction which should be recalled during the remainder of this discussion. A Jewish interpretation is not an evaluation or critique of Christian interpretations. It does not claim to present the one true interpretation of the revelation of Jesus, nor does it imply that Christian interpretations are in error and should be corrected to the Jewish interpretation; i.e., it is not what Christians should necessarily believe. Rather, it is an attempt to find a meaningful interpretation true to Jewish tradition for Jews.

[40] For further discussion on this problem see Franz Mussner, Tractate on the Jews, tr. Leonard Swidler (Philadelphia: Fortress, 1984), pp. 346-353; van Buren, Discerning the Way, p. 172.

[41] Is. 46:11-12, 53; Ps. 116:16; Mac. 7.37-38; 4 Mac. 6:27-29; Shab. 33b; Yoma 38b; Mek. Ex. 12:1; Sif. Num. 25:13; Mid. Ps. 118:18; Ta'an. 8a; M. Katon 28a.

[42] A new problem in talking about resurrection is the range of definitions in both Judaism and Christianity for this concept. The traditional concept of both was bodily resurrection, but this has been rejected by some Jews and Christians. No specific definition for resurrection is necessary for the following discussion. The reader is encouraged to substitute his or her own specific definition for the term. Obviously the primary sources from either Christian or Jewish tradition were referring to a "bodily resurrection," not to be confused with the miraculous resuscitation of the dead by Elisha and Jesus. But this does not mean that their definition for resurrection is necessarily the only correct definition.

[43] Herschel Matt, "How Shall a Believing Jew View Christianity?" Judaism, vol. 24 (1975), pp. 402-403; Lapide, Jewish Monotheism and Christian Trinitarian Doctrine, pp. 59, 67-68.

44 Deut. 32:39; Is. 26:19; Ezek. 37:1-14; Hos. 6:12; Ps. 113:7, 116:4-11, 118:17-18; Job 19:23-27; Dan. 12:2, 13; 2 Mac. 7:9, 12:43; 1 En. 6-36, 65, 83-90; 2 Bar. 30, 50.

45 San. 90a-92a; Shab. 88b; R. Shan. 17a; Ba. Mez. 58b; Ket. 111a, b.

46 Matt, "How Shall a Believing Jew View Christianity?" pp. 402-403; Lapide, Jewish Monotheism and Christianity Trinitarian Doctrine, pp. 67-68.

47 Acts 2:24, 32, 3:15, 26, 4:10, 5:30, 10:40, 13:30-37, 17:31; Rom. 4:24, 6:4, 10:9; 1 Cor. 6:14, 15:15; 2 Cor. 4:14; Gal. 1:11; Eph. 1:20; Col. 2:12; 1 Thes. 1:10; 1 Pet. 1:4.

48 Deut. 4:37, 7:6-9, 10:15; Mid. Ps. 44:1.

49 Ex. 3:11; Is. 6:5; Jer. 1:6.

50 Acts 4:12, 5:30, 10:42, 17:31; Rom. 4:25, 10:5; 1 Thes. 1:10. For a discussion of the view of the resurrection in theocentric terms and the change to the view of the resurrection as proving the divine identity of Jesus see J. Christian Beker, Paul the Apostle (Philadelphia: Fortress, 1980), pp. 152-160.

51 See Mt. 28; Mk. 16; Lk. 24; Acts 1-2, 10-11, 15.

52 Mt. 10:5-6, 15:21-28; Mk. 7:24-30.

53 Mt. 28:16-20; Mk. 16:14-18; Lk. 24:44-48; Acts 1:6-8.

54 Acts 2-4, 6-7, 8:4-14, 10-11, 26:12-18; Gal. 1:15-17, 2:7-10.

55 Acts 1:6-7.

56 Rom. 3:29-30, 4:16-17, 9:24-26, 10:18-20, 11:7-32, 15:8-15; Gal. 3:8-14.

57 Rom. 1:16, 2:10, 3:1-4, 9:4-5, 11:1-32.

58 The existence of Gentile proselytes to Judaism at this time is supported by numerous primary sources, but the extent and support for such Gentile missions is still a matter of debate. For an introduction to the

problem see Mary Smallwood, The Jews under Roman Rule (Leiden: E. J. Brill, 1976), pp. 129-130, 205-213, 376-379; Bernard Bamberger, Proselytism in the Talmudic Period (New York: KTAV, 1968), pp. 135-138; W. G. Braude, Jewish Proselytizing in the First Five Centuries of the Common Era (Providence: Brown University Press, 1940), pp. 137-138; H. Rowley, The Biblical Doctrine of Election (London: Lutterworth, 1950), p. 91; Joseph Bonsirven, Palestinian Judaism in the Time of Jesus Christ (New York: Holt, Rinehart, Winston, 1964), pp. 68-69.

59 Is. 2:2, 19:19-25, 45:20-25, 56:1-8, 66:23; Jer. 3:17, 16:19; Amos 9:7, 12; Zech. 2:11-15, 8:20-23; 14:16; Mic. 4:2.

60 En. 1, 10, 45, 49-50, 60-63, 90-91; Ps. Sol. 17-18; 2 Bar. 17-30, 39-40, 69-74; Tob. 13-14; As. Mos. 8-10; Ap. Ab. 29-30; 4 Ezra 5-7, 12-13; Sib. Or. 3:200, 556-557, 669.

61 Jub. 7:10-14, 10:29-34, 16:7-10, 24:28-30, 35:14; Sib. Or. 3:302-381. See also E. P. Sanders, "The Covenant as a Soteriological Category and the Nature of Salvation in Palestinian and Hellenistic Judaism," in R. Hamerton-Kelly and R. Scroggs, eds., Jews, Greeks, and Christians (Leiden: E. J. Brill, 1976), p. 42; D. Wilhelm Bousset and Hugo Gressman, Die Religion des Judentums in späthellenistischen Zeitalter (Tübingen: J. C. B. Mohr, 1966), p. 304.

62 Jub. 3:31-32, 6:35; 2 Bar. 15:4-6; T. Naph. 3:3, 8:4; 4 Ezra 7:20-22; Pes. Kid. 199b; Sif. Deut. 142b; Num. Rab. 14:20, 32:4. See also Montefiore and Loewe, A Rabbinic Anthology, pp. 78-80.

63 Acts 15:1-29; Gal. 1:6-2:14. See also Lloyd Gaston, "Paul and Torah," in Davies, Anti-Semitism and the Foundations of Christianity, pp. 56-61.

64 This new view is consistent with Acts 21:17-26, 24:10-21, 26:4-23. See also Gaston, "Paul and Torah," p. 66; E. P. Sanders, "Paul's Attitude toward the Jewish People," Union Seminary Quarterly Review, vol. 33 (1978), p. 176; E. P. Sanders, Paul and Palestinian Judaism (Philadelphia: Fortress, 1977), pp. 1-24, 463-472; W. Davies, "Paul and the People of Israel," New Testament Studies, vol. 24 (1977), p. 12; W. Davies, "Paul and the Law," p. 5, and Marna Hooker, "Paul and Covenantal Nomism," p. 49, both in M. Hooker

113

and S. Wilson, eds., <u>Essays in Honour of C. K. Barrett</u> (London: SPCK, 1982); Stendahl, <u>Paul among Jews and Gentiles</u>, p. 2; and Paul van Buren, <u>A Christian Theology of the People Israel</u> (New York: Seabury, 1983), pp. 272-282.

[65] This is, as stated in the discussion, only a tentative answer to the question of why Gentiles should not convert to Judaism. A detailed analysis of this question forms the major portion of the author's dissertation, which is in progress at the present time.

WHY THE DIALOGUE WITH JUDAISM IS INDISPENSABLE FOR CHRISTIAN THEOLOGY

Notes on Jewish-Christian Dialogue

by

Stefan Schreiner

There is no such thing as a dialogue without pre-suppositions. Every dialogue, insofar as it is an authentic dialogue and hopes to succeed, presumes the presence of individual positions on the part of every dialogue partner as well as an attitude which in general can be abbreviated as a readiness for dialogue, an attitude which--without giving up one's own opinion--aims more at allowing oneself to be spoken to than at wishing to speak to the other, an attitude which--without prematurely forsaking one's own opinion--evidences the fundamental readiness to place oneself in question, an attitude which respects the dialogue partner as fundamentally an equal, an attitude which is prepared to affirm at the beginning of the dialogue that its conclusion is fundamentally open. If this is true for every dialogue, it is of course also true for the dialogue between Jews and Christians.

Concerning the requisite attitude A. Geiger over a hundred years ago penned the following sentence, which deserves to be cited in full here:

> In approaching a religion in which we do not participate we must never forget that numerous generations have venerated it as something holy (and continue to do so), in which they sought and found their blessedness, that there are yet today millions who seek shelter under its roof and who believe that they find peace for their souls there; it would be inappropriate and unworthy if we wished to designate the reflections and actions of a professor of this religion as worthy of disdain because we could not likewise approve it, and it would profoundly corrupt us ourselves if we sought in it grounds for hate and polemic.[1]

As presuppositions for a dialogue between Jews and Christians, Abraham Heschel listed in a letter to teachers of the Jewish people in 1959 the following:

> What are the presuppositions for a dialogue between Jews and the Christian world? The most important presupposition for a dialogue between human beings with different faiths is the faith itself. Second, that one opens oneself to the situation of the other human being without concern for his religion. Third, we are obliged [says Abraham Heschel as a Jew!] to acknowledge the mutual relationship between Judaism and Christianity.[2]

That a dialogue with men and women of other faiths or religions carried out under these conditions, that is, characterized by the effort to understand the faith or religion of the other in the same way as the one professing, likewise has an effect on the understanding of one's own faith, one's own religion--indeed, must have--can hardly be surprising. In this regard this reflexive effect can produce equally an enrichment in the sense of a deepening of the understanding of one's own religion, but it can also call forth doubts which in the end lead one to ask whether the opposing position of the other might not in fact be justified. In every case, at any rate, such a dialogue engenders a critical attitude toward one's own faith, one's own religion,[3] until in the end one perceives one's own religion not only as a religious-scientific phenomenon, but also at the same time as a religious-scientific problem, and thereby conceives it, because it concerns one's own religion, as a theological problem, as for example Louis Massignon and E. Faure, and above all H. Corbin have done.[4]

With this we have reached the subject which I would like to handle in the following in three sections. In the first we must deal with Christianity as a religious-scientific phenomenon (and thereby as a religious-scientific problem, to take up the above-mentioned terminology once again). From this we wish to investigate the necessities, but even more so the possibilities, which flow therefrom for an understanding of Christianity through an encounter with Judaism. Finally, we shall make an attempt to describe the relationship of Judaism and Christianity to one another, their being alongside of and over against each other.

I.

If one observes Christianity and how in its early witnesses as well as its later developments as churches and confessions presents totally different images, there are nevertheless two essential components which have marked it unto this very day, namely, the Jewish heritage and the Greek, or rather, Hellenistic, heritage. As this is so of course is no cause for wonder if one recalls that the first Christians were Jews and that those who made Christianity into Christianity on the other hand were Greeks/Hellenists.

Both heritages of course need to be more precisely differentiated, for one can no more speak of the Jewish heritage than of the Judaism as a firmly defined unified entity at the time of the development of the early church and the New Testament writings. The corresponding is also of course true for the Hellenistic heritage, for there is also no single Hellenistic heritage.

Without wishing or even being able here to go into details, it would be well to mention summarily those components which from the Jewish heritage have been of determining significance for developing Christianity. K. Rudolf, who I follow here, summarized these components in the following fashion:

> 1. The Israelite-Jewish concept of God, doubtless the most fundamental presupposition for the rise of Christianity.

> 2. The Old Testament prophets who in one of their last representatives, John the Baptist, were the immediate model of Jesus of Nazareth. . . .

> 3. The apocalyptic with its eschatological-messianic view of history and prophetic "futurology," its dualistic cosmology and anthropology. . . .

117

4. The "intensification of the Torah" on the part of contemporary Jewish radicalism, as it is portrayed for us in the Qumran writings and took on a striking significance for the ethics of Jesus, and finally of Christianity.

5. The dualistic wisdom teaching, an area which in most recent times is coming into increasing focus both as concerning primitive and early Christianity . . . as well as gnosticism.

6. The Jewish esoteric and gnosis, which to be sure were not central or what ultimately became the official standard of Christianity, but which nevertheless were of significance in the rise and development of Christian gnosticism, and have left indestructable traces, as the Johannine and Pauline traditions or "schools" show forth. . . .[5]

As was understandable and natural, Christianity which was thus so influenced developed at first as nothing other than a Jewish sect with a specific messianic direction. The later division between Judaism and Hellenism which became so important is in the first instance a result of the missionary practice, and the thereto most closely connected change in attitude toward the Jewish religious law, as one may well perceive in the debate between Peter and Paul (Gal. 2:11-14; Acts 15:1-29). It certainly was not called forth by the problem of Judaism or the problem of Hellenism. While Jewish Christianity conserved the traditions of the primitive Jerusalem community, Hellenistic Christianity opened itself to the influences of the surrounding world--and that meant the non-Jewish surrounding world--to such a degree that it had to pay the price of the loss or the giving up of the task of the older, Jewish, heritage of faith. In this development Paul plays a part, which J. Leipoldt clearly had seen.[6] Also, H. Conzelmann certainly was right when he discerned a break between the primitive Jerusalem community and the Hellenistic church.[7] For it was only through Christianity's leap to the extra-Palestinian universal empire that it became a shaping and establishing religion alongside and outside of Judaism, and then a world-embracing church--it was the Hellenistic heritage[8] which gave Christianity, the church, its decisive shape. Indeed, one may without doubt maintain that had Christianity not accomplished this it would presumably have remained a Jewish-messianic sect--the evidence for which Shlomo Pines laid out several years ago.[9] This Christianity would have been comparable in its significance perhaps to the Dönme sect in Turkey.[10]

The leap into the extra-Palestinian world did not necessitate Christianity's, the church's, complete giving up of its Jewish heritage, but it probably demanded and initiated a far-reaching--and the expression is proper here--Christianization of this Jewish heritage which now underwent a profound meta-morphosis. To be sure, in order to be somewhat more concrete, almost all of the theological concepts which came from the Jewish heritage were retained; however, they were at the same time filled with complementary, new content: for example, from biblical monotheism there developed trinitarian dogma, and from Messianol-ogy there developed Christology, etc. The here-indicated process of giving a new meaning, a trans-formed meaning, is clearly enough discernible in the writings of the New Testament. The entrance of Judaism into the Hellenistic world is in this regard, there-fore, not comparable with the entrance of Christianity into the Hellenistic world. As Y. Amir accurately formulated the matter, for the former it meant "the stimulation of thought arose from the foreign element, while that which was thought, in a monumental new for-mulation, came from the native element."[11] For the latter, however, that is, Christianity, in keeping with Amir's formulation, it was not only the stimulation of thought that came from the foreign elements, but at the same time that which was thought also came from the foreign element; the native element at most appeared as the native element adapted to the foreign.

Not only the New Testament scriptures belong to the holy scriptures of Christianity, but also just as much the so-called Old Testament, the Jewish Bible. That means that the Jewish heritage is, to the present day, visibly present in a double manner within Chris-tianity: it is present for one in the form of the Hebrew scriptures of the Bible, and for another it is present not in a specific figure, but rather in the Greek scriptures of the Bible as a "monumental new formulation." Already, in this placing alongside one another of the Old and New Testaments alone the problem of continuity and discontinuity between Judaism and Christianity is reflected; the conflict between the Jewish heritage in Christianity and its Christianized form is reflected precisely in the problem of Paul in Romans 9-11.

To sum up what has been said to this point: Christianity is therefore both in continuity and discontinuity in regard to Judaism. From this it follows that in its continuity with Judaism Christianity is ununderstandable without a knowledge of Judaism; on the other hand, in its discontinuity it is probably understandable without a knowledge of Judaism, but not without a knowledge of the Hellenistic world and its culture--but here, this latter problem will not concern us further.

II.

If, therefore, Christianity exhibits a continuity with Judaism, we then have to ask what an encounter with Judaism can contribute to the understanding of Christianity. This appears to me to be divisible into three parts:

a) An encounter with Judaism provides first of all a necessary, indispensable help to an intellectual understanding of Christianity. Every attempt to grasp Christianity at its origin and its first beginnings is necessarily directed toward an encounter with Judaism. Without a knowledge of that which is usually referred to as "the Jewish background of the New Testament" the life, actions and teachings of the man Jesus of Nazareth are not understandable. Neither are his encounters with the scribal authorities of his time nor the reactions of those around him to him and to his behavior, nor indeed the discussion between Peter and Paul, nor the debates between the first Christians and the early church with the Judaism of its time--in a word, nothing of all that which the New Testament gives witness to, including all the related theological con- ceptual apparatus, is at all understandable.

However, in addition, without a knowledge of Judaism--and this is unfortunately very often over- looked--the so-called Old Testament is fundamentally also not really understandable, for the canon of the Hebrew scriptures of the Bible is indeed no accidental

120

result but rather is the product of the theological judgment of Jewish scholars of ancient times. Moreover, not only was the canon fixed by Jewish scholars, but also the vocalization system which gives the Hebrew text a specific pronunciation and reading, the result of centuries-long exegetical work by Jewish scholars. And it is precisely this scriptural canon that the church has taken over and raised up to an indispensable part of its holy scriptures! To be sure, the church did not take over the canon of the Hebrew scriptures as the Jewish Bible, but rather under the perspective of a responding exegetical methodology and the understanding of the text attained through it, namely, that of the Christian Old Testament--which R. J. Zwi Werblowsky once described by insisting that the Tanak and the Old Testament are not the same thing! That, however, changes nothing of the fact that a desire for an authentic understanding of this part of the Christian Bible presumes that one knows why the Jewish scholars decided for the canon as we know it, that one knows on the basis of what exegetical insights and traditions the Masoretes have vocalized the text. That here very conscious decisions were made is quite discernible in a series of Ketivs and Qeres (for example, Job 13:15!). At times the knowledge of the Jewish exegetical traditions is the only thing that makes it possible to understand a particular text (for example, Jer. 25:26, 51:1; Is. 29:22; Ezek. 5:7, 11:12).[12]

In distinction to the New Testament, however, in which the Jewish heritage is present only in a "revised form," the so-called Old Testament retains the pure Jewish heritage. This is made obvious already in the constant battle throughout the history of the church and theology concerning the place of the Old Testament within the Christian church. This Old Testament, however, is an always-present Jewish challenge against every attempt to formulate a theology, a Christian theological doctrine, without contact with the Jewish tradition. From this standpoint it is merely thoroughly consistent thought when someone like Adolf von Harnack (who was neither the first nor the last to do so) demanded:

> The rejection of the Old Testament in the second century was a mistake which the great church correctly rejected; to hold fast to this in the sixteenth century was a fate it was not yet able to avoid; but to retain

it as the canonical original proclamation in Protestantism since the
nineteenth century is the result of a
religious and ecclesiastical
crippling. . . . To make a clean
sweep of things here and to give the
truth the place of honor in confession and instruction, that is the
great deed which today--almost too
late--is demanded of Protestantism.[13]

With this we would have already arrived at the
difficulties which the encounter with Judaism can present. However, let us remain with the possibilities
which it opens up, for:

b) Along with the necessity mentioned, such an
encounter offers an expansion of the horizon which I
would likewise like to designate as necessary, which
signifies something more than a merely intellectual
enrichment (which of course already is a great deal).
This is a necessary expansion of the horizon because it
allows and helps the suppressed or forgotten dimensions
of the biblical-theological substance to be discovered
once again.

To study the biblical commentaries of the rabbis,
the midrashim, etc., has without any doubt its own
special attraction. Even if we can no longer accept
all of their hermeneutical and exegetical rules and
methods for explaining the scriptures, their exegesis,
their "creative philology" (I. Heinemann) is often
extremely stimulating and eye-opening. Their keen eye
for fine details sometimes enables surprising connections to be opened up. These exegetes have in particular a freedom in dealing with the scriptures which
presumes that for a single biblical verse there is not
just one, but, as it says in the Talmud (bSanh 34a),
there can indeed be seventy exegeses of which not only
one is correct and the other sixty nine are classified
as false--abstracting completely from the fact that the
Talmud knows of no teaching authority which had made
such a decision or could make such a decision.[14]

There should also at least be mention made here of
the possibility of giving familiar concepts and texts a
fullness of meaning through an inquiring into the
Jewish tradition, which can mean a spiritual and intellectual deepening of their content, which Peter von der
Osten-Sacken has shown in exemplary fashion with the

examples he provides in his book <u>Katechismus</u> <u>und</u>
<u>Siddur</u>.[15]

c) The encounter with Judaism can, however, also
be the occasion of difficulties and hide "dangers" in
itself, namely, there where through it it becomes clear
how far Christianity, above all in its doctrine, has
throughout the course of its historical development
moved away from its Jewish origins and roots--namely,
there where through the Jewish dialogue partner the
discrepancy between origin and development becomes
evident. There the encounter with Judaism fulfills the
function of an objection, a contradiction and a corrective. It prevents Christianity from turning from a
biblical religion of revelation into a Hellenistic
philosophy. The encounter with Judaism is an inquiry
into the loyalty to the Bible by Christianity and its
teachings. It makes possible the stimulation of
reflection on, for example, what has happened to the
monotheistic confession (Dt. 6:4ff.) as it was turned
into a trinitarian dogma, or what sort of a metamor-
phosis the biblical decalogue underwent until it could
become a part of Luther's catechism, or how the prophetic, messianic preacher of repentance, the Jewish
teacher, Jesus of Nazareth, could be made into a
founding figure from whom the movement which had been
started by him could become an independent religion
which transcended the ground and limits of Judaism--in
a word: how Christianity and Judaism, despite its
daughter-mother relationship, could become two divided
religions, each existing for themselves (despite all of
the existing mutual existential relationships between
them, of which Abraham Heschel spoke); indeed, the
daughter religion was able ultimately to express its
own self only in distinction from the mother religion

The fact that Christianity and Judaism very soon
were recognized and seen to be essentially quite different from each other is indicated not leastwise by
the introduction of the <u>birkat</u> <u>ha-minim</u> into the
twelfth <u>Berakhah</u> of the Eighteen Prayer, which
according to bBer 28b should be attributed to
R. Gamliel II (therefore, around 100 C.E.). This
<u>birkat</u> <u>ha-minim</u> excluded Jewish-Christians (as well as
other sectarians) from the Jewish community. Hellenistic Christians in any case were never looked upon as
members of the Jewish community.

At this point it might be well to insert some
remarks on the topic of Jewish-Christians, concerning

whom today there again is a great deal of talk, not least probably also because they themselves speak about themselves.[16] To be sure, there was a Jewish-Christianity as a historical religious phenomenon; H. J. Schoeps, J. Danielou, S. Pines and others have presented it and described it for us. However, the moment that this religious community disappeared sometime during the Middle Ages, Jewish-Christianity likewise ceased to exist. To speak of Jewish-Christianity today suggests the possibility that one can be a Jew and a Christian at the same time. However, in this one forgets that a Jew who confesses her or himself to be a Christian *ipso* *facto* ceases to be a Jew, unless one defines being a Jew--horribile dictu!--in a racist sense as the Nuremberg laws of 1935 did. The reflections of Peter von der Osten-Sacken on a kind of middle position for Jewish-Christians between Jews and Christians[17] are really not acceptable. That is still likewise true when one affirms that ultimately we have the New Testament only thanks to Jewish-Christians. However, were these people really still Jews, as they believed in Jesus now no longer only as the Messiah but honored him as God? Perhaps one would rather have to describe the New Testament as a book by converts, with all of the problems that lie in that concept. Paul, for example, was not only an apostle but likewise also an apostate, and he probably had to be an apostate in order to become the apostle which he likewise was.[18]

With this we have arrived at our third point, namely, an attempt to describe the relationship between Judaism and Christianity and to formulate a goal for the Jewish-Christian dialogue.

III.

In this attempt we proceed from the fact which cannot be dismissed, namely, that Judaism and Christianity, despite all of the mutually existing existential relationships between them--in order once again to take up the formulation of Abraham Heschel--are two different religions and ways of believing which are divided from each other, and a blurring of the demarcation lines between them consequently must be and will be excluded, not least of all because of intellectual honesty, if the encounter, the dialogue, is to make sense for both partners and is to succeed. For the goals of this dialogue can and may not be either a rejudaization of Christianity or a christianization of Judaism. That a clarification of the relationship between Judaism and Christianity which strives for a truly new relationship between the two is urgently needed is shown by the present discussion, which has thereby been called into existence--and the longer it is continued the clearer this need becomes. In particular the inner-Christian controversies, as they have broken out especially in the aftermath of the conclusion of the Rhineland Synod of January, 1980,[19] press for a clarification of the important contents and demands. I mention here only the key terms: "two paths of salvation--yes or no," "mission to the Jews--yes or no," "giving up of Christian fundamental truths because of a bad conscience in light of our own history," etc. I cannot and do not wish to go further into these controversies here. I wish only to ask whether the ways to find and give answers to the questions thus raised, whether an ever more subtle exegesis of Paul, for example, or an ever more committed return to the sources, that is, an ever more uncompromising return to the beginning of Christianity--however important these researches also are, as mentioned above--whether these efforts really change things in the relationship between Jews and Christians today, that is, whether they are able to improve the relationship. To me it is a very large question whether or not one can go behind historical happenings, even when one is in a position to show that they were dependent upon mistaken interpretations or misunderstandings.

To my mind a very beautiful image of the possible relationship between Judaism and Christianity was described by Claude Montefiore when he said that (enlightened) Jews and (enlightened) Christians sometime, someplace in the middle will reach out their hands in friendship to each other, though each will remain with their own "commitment."[20]

In fact every religion makes an absolute claim in view of what it confesses and cannot give it up if it does not wish to give itself up. The question is only if this absoluteness is to be understood as an extensive one, therefore also including other human beings, or as an intensive one, therefore making claims of validity only for the confessor of the specific religion. For me only the second form of a claim of absoluteness is acceptable, and if I understand the matter rightly, then the doctrine of the Noachide commandments, together with its consequences, has within Judaism precisely the task of justifying this second form of absoluteness, the intensive absoluteness, without having thereby to undermine the fundament of its own religion, biblical monotheism.[21]

Every claim of absoluteness naturally bases itself on a claim to truth. Hence, it is necessary that a number of reflections on truth in the world of religion be made here. Here truth always first of all means divine reality and at bottom only this: "The seal of the Holy One, may he be praised, is truth" (bShabbat 51a). The Islamic mystics have reserved their Arabic word for truth exclusively for God: God is truth. This indicates that truth ultimately is something which has been withdrawn from human disposition. Such truth can only be experienced and wishes to be conserved. Concerning this truth one can say something only when one has encountered it, when one has experienced it. "Can you prove God through research?" asked Job (11:7) and affirmed: "Behold, God is greater (El saggi) than we understand" (36:26)! The same doubtless is implied in the confessional shout "Allahu akbar!" God is greater!

This concept of truth of course is to be distinguished from that truth which, for example, is asked about in the famous question of Pilate (Jn. 18:38),[22] that is, the truth which a religious statement claims for itself. In this a religious statement means a statement which a human being makes concerning the divine reality after encountering it. For those who make such a statement it is naturally true in all circumstances; for them it rests on the accepted de facto identity of the content of the statement with the divine reality itself which has been spoken (for example, God is self-revealed in Christ!).

It becomes problematic when the subject of such a religious statement is left out of consideration. For then the religious statement becomes a doctrinal statement which claims to be true now no longer simply subjectively but also objectively. Eric Fromm described this development in a very effective way as the alienation of a concept:

> When the concept is alienated, that is, when it is separated from the experience to which it is related, it thereby loses its reality and is transformed into an artificial figure of the human spirit. Through this there arises the fiction that every-

one who uses the <u>concept</u> thereby relates himself to the <u>experience</u> which as a substratum underlies it. As soon as this happens . . . an idea which gives expression to an experience is transformed into an <u>ideology</u> which sets itself in place of the reality which lies at the basis of living human beings.[23]

That has as a consequence that the religious statement which has become doctrine, because it now makes the claim to be true also in an objective sense, declares every different sounding statement to be heresy, and consequently must deny its having the content of truth. As a consequence this means nothing less than an attempt to enclose the divine reality, God, within a conceptual statement, which in the end makes of God something to be disposed of and indeed prescribes for God when, where and how God is self-revealed to a human being. This always happens where, for example, statements such as in Acts 4:12 or Jn. 14:6 are no longer exegeted in the sense of the above-defined religious statements but rather as doctrine. In this latter case there is in fact no place for another religious statement. Such an attempt ultimately does not take the divinity of God seriously any longer in that it says to God, indeed, precisely prescribes for God, the possibilities of addressing a human being. Such an attempt, in my opinion, is connected with human <u>hubris</u> in an intimate way and is unacceptable.

If, as a consequence, God's possibilities of self-revelation to human beings are multiple, as I personally am convinced, then I gladly admit that I reject the understanding or indeed the defense of a mission whose goal is to persuade human beings to come over to another belief. "If God had willed, he could have made all of you into one community" (Sura 5, 49/53); however, "He has set each one of you on the path on which he finds himself" (2, 148/3), says the Qur'an—and with it I am in full agreement. That of course is not to say that for me there is more than one path. For me also there is only one path; however, by the very fact that I claim this path for myself, I wish at the same time to provide room for the same right for another, namely, that for him or her there is only the one other path and that he or she wishes to remain therein; as Moses Mendelssohn once stated: "We indeed believe that our religion is the best because we hold it to be divine. However, from this it does not follow that it is the best _per_ _se_. It is the best for us and our descendants."

If the dialogue, the encounter, with Judaism, is to have any meaning, then it can only signify, in my opinion, not the recognition of a second or a third or . . . path, but rather the acceptance and recognition that the other persons have their own paths to God which I must attempt to understand, or at least must be ready to do so. Because everyone renders an accounting to others concerning their own religious belief-- indeed, that is the task of theology--both learn not only to understand one another, but in the process also simultaneously gain a deepened understanding of their own faith. A dialogue which is carried on with the presuppositions laid out at the beginning of this essay will enrich both dialogue partners in an equal degree. And if it is successful, there can arise in the end from the mutual inquiry a common search.

> Whether Jew, whether Christian: there is only one
>   God.
> However, humanity seeks God under many names.
> When we stand before God, God does not ask
> by which pilgrim path we have come.

Mascha Kaléko

Translated by

Leonard Swidler

[1] A. Geiger, Vorlesungen über das Judenthum und seine Geschichte (Berlin, 1875), Theil III, p. 94.

[2] Quoted by Y. Aschkenazy, "Mein Weg nach Bad Neuenahr," in B. Klappert and H. Starck, eds., Umkehr und Erneuerung, Erläuterungen zum Synodalbeschluss der Rheinischen Landessynode 1980 (Neukirchen, 1980), p. 2.

[3] K. Rudolph spoke in this connection of the "Ideology Critical Function of Religionswissenschaft," Numen, vol. 25 (1978), pp. 17-39.

[4] Cf. U. Schoen, Das Ereignis und die Antworten. Auf der Suche nach einer Theologie der Religionen heute (Göttingen, 1984).

[5] K. Rudolph, "Das frühe Christentum als religionsgeschichtliches Phänomen," in J. Irmscher and K. Treu, eds., Das Korpus der Griechischen Christlichen Schriftsteller (Berlin, 1977; TU 120), pp. 29-42, 53.

[6] J. Leipoldt, Von den Mysterien zur Kirche (Leipzig, 1961), pp. 62ff., 67ff., 214ff., 218ff.

[7] H. Conzelmann, Geschichte des Urchristentums, 2nd ed. (Göttingen, 1972), p. 53.

[8] For a characterization of it see Rudolph, "Das frühe Christentum," pp. 34-36.

[9] S. Pines, The Jewish Christians of the Early Centuries of Christianity according to a New Source (Jerusalem, 1966).

[10] Cf. G. Scholem, Die jüdische Mystik in ihren Hauptströmungen (Frankfurt/M., 1968), p. 332.

[11] Y. Amir, "Wie verarbeitte das Judentum fremde Einflüsse in hellenistischer Zeit," Judaica, vol. 38 (1982), p. 161.

[12] Cf. M. J. Mulder, "Der Wert der altjüdischen Exegese für die christlichexegetische Arbeit," Judaica, vol. 37 (1981), pp. 129-147.

[13] A. von Harnack, Marcion, 2nd ed. (Leipzig, 1924), pp. 127, 222.

[14] Cf. the noteworthy details provided by J. J. Petuchowski, in his Wie unsere Meister die Schrift erklären. Beispielhafte Bibelauslegung aus dem Judentum (Freiburg-Vienna-Basel, 1982), pp. 134-135.

[15] P. von der Osten-Sacken, Katechismus und Siddur. Aufbrüche mit Martin Luther und den Lehrern Israels, Veröffentlichungen aus dem Institut Kirche und Judentum 15 (Berlin-Munich, 1984).

[16] Cf. K. Kjaer-Hansen and O. Chr. M. Kvarme, Messianische Juden. Juden-christen in Israel, Erlanger Taschenbücher 67 (Erlangen, 1983), as well as my review in Theologische Literaturzeitung, vol. 109 (1984), cols. 805-807.

[17] P. von der Osten-Sacken, Grundzüge einer Theologie im christlich-jüdischen Gespräch, Abhandlungen zum jüdisch-christlichen Dialog 12 (Munich, 1982).

[18] Cf. M. Barth, J. Blank, J. Bloch, F. Mussner, R. J. Zwi Werblowski, Paulus--Apostat oder Apostel. Jüdische und christliche Antworten (Regensburg, 1977).

[19] Cf. note 2 above; Leonard Swidler, "Germany, Christianity and the Jews: From Diatribe to Dialogue," in this volume, and the Ecumenical Press Service Documentation No. 42 (Frankfurt/M., 1980); the amount of critical literature is almost overwhelming. A comprehensive documentation is being prepared by E. Brocke and J. Seim, eds.

[20] Quoted in Zeichen der Zeit, vol. 9 (1982), p. 210.

[21] For this information and the following cf. G. Mensching, Toleranz und Wahrheit in der Religion, Siebenstern Taschenbuch 81 (Munich-Hamburg, 1966).

[22] One should attend to the different uses of the word "truth" in Jn. 18:37 (Jesus gives witness to the truth, i.e., God) and Jn. 18:38 (Pilate does not ask who, but what, truth is).

[23] E. Fromm, Ihr werdet sein wie Gott (Reinbeck b. Hamburg, 1980), pp. 18-19.

IMPLICATIONS OF RECENT RESEARCH ON THE PHARISEES
FOR JEWISH-CHRISTIAN DIALOGUE

by

Lewis John Eron

I. INTRODUCTION

Ellis Rivkin calls his book on the Pharisees <u>A Hidden Revolution</u>.[1] The book's title accurately describes what can, without a doubt, be known about Pharisaism--that is, the Pharisees were an important group in Palestine in the first centuries B.C.E. and C.E. who contributed to the development of Rabbinic Judaism, and were able to hide their traces so well that the details and history of their contribution has remained hidden.

The Pharisees appear to be an important group in the first-century Jewish matrix in Palestine, out of which early Christianity and Rabbinic Judaism grew. Our basic sources,[2] Josephus, the New Testament, and Rabbinic literature, although they do not present a mutually consistent picture, all seem to support such a view. For Josephus, the Pharisees are a political party supported by the masses, with a distinct religious platform. For the New Testament, the Pharisees are the opponents of Jesus who are obsessed with the meticulous performance of the details of Jewish Law and out of touch with the common folk. For Rabbinic literature, the Pharisees are the wise and pious predecessors of the Rabbis, ethical teachers and interpreters of revelation.

The controversies between Jesus and the Pharisees as reported in the Gospels form the first group in the polemic relationship between Judaism and Christianity.[3] Yet the particular importance of the Pharisees for Jewish-Christian dialogue today stems from a basic change in the way Christian scholars approached Judaism that occurred at the end of the nineteenth century. Previously, the approach was to stress the similarities between the two religions with the intent of showing that Judaism, if understood correctly, points to Christianity. The new approach emphasized the discontinuity between Judaism and Christianity. In a chain of tradition that began with F. Weber and included such luminaries as Bousset and Schürer, Billerbeck and Bultmann,

Judaism was presented as a dry legalistic religion with an inaccessible God. Christianity, on the other hand, was a religion that stressed faith over works and had a loving, ever-present Diety.[4] Pharisaism, identified with Judaism, stood out as a dead religion.[5]

Positive evaluations of Pharisaism written in the same period by Anglo-American scholars such as George Foot Moore, R. T. Herford, S. Schecter and C. G. Montifiore did not have the same impact.

E. P. Sanders attributes the failure of the positive evaluation of the Pharisees to become the standard Christian view to a number of factors. They include the problems of language, German versus English, as well as the apparent underpinning given to Weber's understanding of the Pharisees by Billerbeck's Kommentar zum Neuen Testament aus Talmud und Midrash.[6] In addition, the differences between Moore's position and that of Weber, Bousset, Schürer, Billerbeck, etc., were not clearly drawn. G. F. Moore did not polemicize in his master work, Judaism in the First Centuries of the Christian Era: The Age of the Tannaim (1927-1930), but restricted his criticism of German scholarship to a journal article.[7] Thus, students of Moore's work were not made aware of the issues.

In addition, most Christian theologians and scholars obtained their knowledge of Judaism in the context of their seminary education. Therefore, they were more likely to be influenced by the "German" school, who were New Testament scholars, than by the "Anglo-American" scholars, who, with the exception of Montifiore, a Jew, were not. Antisemitism on both sides of the Atlantic in the nineteenth and twentieth centuries was also a contributing factor.

In recent years, there has been a trend to re-evaluate the Pharisees and their relationship to Jesus and early Christianity. In part, this is due to a growing awareness of the devastating results of traditional Christian anti-Judaism. This awareness forms part of the background for all contemporary Jewish-Christian dialogue. The first recognizable step in the reevaluation took place on the level of church councils and their pronouncements. It was followed shortly thereafter by developments in religious education as well as in studies by theologians and scholars particularly concerned with the rebuilding of relationships between Judaism and Christianity.[8]

Michael J. Cook sees four other factors as important in contemporary interest in the Pharisees. They are: (1) the recognition of the importance of the Pharisees in the growth of modern Judaism, (2) growing familiarity with Rabbinic sources on the part of Christian scholars, (3) the entry of Jewish scholars into New Testament studies, and (4) the lack of a scholarly consensus.[9] It is this lack of consensus that forms the focus of this essay.

The study of the Pharisees is important for other reasons besides those of Jewish-Christian relations. First, it is of general interest for the history of the development of Western religions: Judaism, Christianity, Islam. Second, for Christians, it provides the background for Jesus of Nazareth and can help cast light on the reality of his life. Third, for Jews, the study of the Pharisees is an important part in producing a picture of the developing theology of Rabbinic Judaism.[10]

The problems involved in the study of the Pharisees are immense. They involve the ability to handle critically a wide variety of texts in Hebrew, Aramaic and Greek that not only contradict each other but are also self-contradictory. The source material is temporally and/or geographically removed from the Pharisees. Paul, the only pre-70 C.E. source, writes as a Hellenistic Jew from beyond the borders of Palestine, and the rest of the evidence was edited, if not written, after the failure of the First Jewish Revolt against Rome (73 C.E.). The leading scholars do not agree on basic issues of definition and methodology. Even the meaning of the word "Pharisees" is obscure.[11]

As of now, there is no one answer to the question, "Who were the Pharisees?" In the next section, I will consider briefly the work of four English-speaking scholars--two Jews and two Christians--who have recently studied the issue. I will discuss their results and their methods and evaluate briefly how their work contributes to Jewish-Christian dialogue. This will be followed by a general evaluation.

II. FOUR APPROACHES

A. John Bowker: "Good and Bad Pharisees"

John Bowker, a British scholar, in his book <u>Jesus and the Pharisees</u>,[12] attempts to provide an introduction to the study of the Pharisees. The bulk of his work is a collection of the basic nonbiblical sources on the Pharisees in English translation. As a guide to the material, Bowker provides a fifty-two-page introduction, in which he sketches out his understanding of the issues, as well as traditional notes explaining the controversy between the Sadducees and the Pharisees.

Bowker's concerns are: (1) to explain the rise of the Pharisaic movement, (2) to explain the transition of the term Pharisees/<u>perushim</u> from a possible good sense to a condemnatory sense in Rabbinic literature and (3) to use this new understanding to explain Jesus' relationship with the Pharisees as reported in Mark's Gospel and in the accounts of Jesus' trial.

In his understanding of the rise of the Pharisaic movement, Bowker depends primarily on Josephus. The earliest occurence of the name Pharisees in a historical context is the break with John Hyrcanus (Ant. XIII 288-300, see also Qid. 66a). From this it appears that the Pharisees were already an established group, perhaps connected with the Hasidim of the Maccabean revolt.

Josephus provides incidental information concerning the Pharisees (Ant. XIII 171-3, Ant. XVIII 2-17, 23, War II 118-119) in his discussions of the various Jewish sects: the Pharisees, the Sadducees and the Essenes. The Pharisees are a group with a commitment to the laws and bearers of traditions. They believe in the immortality of the soul and a future new life. They take an intermediate view, allowing both fate and human will. They are cooperative with each other and enjoy the good will of the people, and worship in the Temple is conducted according to their views.

Bowker accepts the identification of the <u>hakamim</u>, the sages, with the Pharisees. He recognizes that there is no uniform usage of the Hebrew term <u>perushim</u> in Rabbinic literature. Sometimes the term is used in a positive sense, and at times in a negative sense. In controversies between the <u>perushim</u> and other groups, especially the Saducees, the perushim and hakamim hold identical views.

In other cases, the perushim are attacked in Rabbinic sources. In J. Ber. 2.4, the perushim are considered the minim, "heretics," referred to in the blessing over the minim in the Standing Prayer, the Amida. The Mishnah reports the saying of R. Joshua, that four things wear out the world: a foolish saint, a wicked man with cunning, a woman who is a prushah and the makkot perushim—the wounds of the perushim (Sot. 3.4).

The Jerusalem Talmud describes makkot perushim as the use of fine points in the Law to go around the intent of the Law (J. Sot. 3.4). Finally, seven types of perushim are mentioned in the Babylonian Talmud in explanation of makkot perushim, and are described in a negative light (B. Sot. 22a, b; see also J. Ber. 9.5). The only perushim who avoid condemnation are the perush from love and the perush from fear.

Bowker explains this phenomena by referring to the possible meanings of the root p-r-s, "to separate." On the one hand, perushim has the positive connotation of those who separate for purposes of holiness. On the other hand, perushim can mean merely "separatists." This may have a neutral meaning, to refer to those who separated from John Hyrcanus and went to the opposition party, to the Saducees.

It also, according to Bowker, developed a negative meaning, "extremists." Bowker understands the negative use of perushim in Rabbinic sources in this light. The Rabbis use perushim to condemn those who take the Rabbis' program of sanctification by the avoidance of uncleanness to uncontrolled extremes. There were divisions among the Pharisees, and strict and lenient views were allowed, as seen in the positions of the schools of Hillel and Shammai. The haburah, association, was for those who wished to be more meticulous. Yet, there were those who went to the extremes and were condemned.

Bowker considers the extremists to be the group that came in conflict with Jesus. The difficulty we have in identifying the Pharisees in Mark's Gospel, commonly taken as the earliest Gospel, is that Mark was writing in the period of transition from the positive Pharisees of Josephus to the negative Pharisees of the Rabbis. The Pharisees involved in the trial of Jesus

135

with the Herodians (Mk. 12:13) were those extremists who removed themselves from the hakamic movement. Cut off from the religious courts controlled by the haka- mim, they participated in the extraordinary proceedings of the Herodians.

Bowker is the least critical of the scholars I will consider. He treats all the sources as if they were contemporary with each other and of equal reli- ability. This is a difficult assumption when one deals with such a variety of materials as he does. Due to this approach, he has the tendency to harmonize the material. This is seen most clearly in his attempt to explain both the positive and negative uses of the term Pharisees/perushim.

He realizes that the Gospel evidence is the result of controversy between Jesus and his followers and the Pharisees, and wisely does not take it as normative. He is less critical in dealing with Josephus and the Rabbis.

Nevertheless, Bowker's essay has important impli- cations, not the least being his collection of the important sources. He understands Judaism in this period as a developing religion, and that Jesus and his early followers interacted with a changing, not static, Judaism. He reminds us of the negative use of the term perushim by the Rabbis themselves and tries to fit the negative presentation of the Pharisees in the New Testament within a Jewish context. He points out the Jewish roots of a now Gentile church and bravely tackles the difficult question of the trial of Jesus. His reconstruction of the history of Pharisaism is flawed deeply, however, by his uncritical approach to the sources.

B. Ellis Rivkin: "Pharisees as Champions of the Twofold Law"

Ellis Rivkin[13] sees the Pharisees as a political and social movement committed to an interpretation of Judaism based on what he calls the twofold law, that is, the written Torah and the oral tradition. The Pharisees developed the ideological/philosophical basis for Western religion. Rivkin presents this as a triad consisting of: "(1) the singular father God so loved the individual that he (2) revealed, through Moses, his twofold law which, if internalized and steadfastly ad- hered to, (3) would gain for such an individual eternal

life for his soul and resurrection for his body."[14] It
is the middle term of this triad that separates Judaism
from Christianity. In Christianity, it is not the
revealed twofold law that was to be internalized but
the Jesus revealed as Christ.

The strengths and the weaknesses of Rivkin's
approach stem from his historical approach.[16] He is
concerned more with the problems of periodization,
structure, process of change, causality and the explanation of change than he is with detailed textual analysis or theological questions.

His major and most controversial contribution is
his definition of the Pharisees from Tannaitic sources,
that is, Mishnah, Tosephta, the Tannaitic midrashim, as
well as baraitot, Tannaitic passages in the two
Talmuds. For Rivkin, it is clear that the term
perushim in Rabbinic literature is not self-defining.
The perushim of Tosef. Ber. 3.25, who are identified as
minim, "heretics," cannot be identical with perushim/
hakamim, whom the rabbis seem to recognize as their
predecessors.

Rivkin rejects the identification of the Pharisees
as a group concerned with issues of purity. He rejects
as evidence M. Hag. 2:7, which lists various levels of
purity, because of the ambiguous use of the word
perushim in the mishnah. The text reads, in part, as
follows: "The garments of an am ha-aretz count as suffering midras uncleanness for perushim; the garments of
perushim count as suffering midras--uncleanness for
them that eat Heave-offering . . ."

The problem is that the Hebrew word perushim can
be either a proper or a common noun, and it is not
clear in which way it is being used in this mishnah.

Rivkin seeks a way of defining the perushim in
Tannaitic literature based on criteria and standards
within the literature itself. He therefore divides all
the references to perushim into three categories.

The first he calls "unambiguous texts," that is,
texts in which the word perushim can only be a proper
noun. These are texts in which the perushim are juxtaposed to zedukim, "Sadducees," for zedukim in Hebrew is
only a proper noun. He expands the corpus of unambiguous texts by incorporating texts which contain words
that are synonymous with perushim and/or zedukim in

137

texts he already examined. In this way, Rivkin is able to make the identification of the perushim with the hakamim, the sages, and the soferim, the Scribes. His conclusions are that the perushim-hakamim-soferim are the champions of the twofold law, and their opponents are the zedukim--Boethusians who adhere to only the written law.[17]

The second category Rivkin calls control texts. These are texts where the term perushim occurs but cannot be translated as Pharisees and given the same definition as perushim in the unambiguous texts.[18] For example, one is T. Ber. 3.25, where the perushim are identified as minim, "heretics." The control texts indicate that the term perushim can be used to describe: heretics, ascetics and separatists, that is, the word can be used for Pharisees and anti-Pharisees.[19]

The third and final category is that of the ambiguous texts. These are texts in which the term perushim is not juxtaposed with zedukim but could be taken as either a common or proper noun. In his review of these texts, Rivkin finds that in these perushim function differently than in the unambiguous texts: (1) They are juxtaposed with am ha-aretz and not zedukim; (2) they are subject to halakhah, "Jewish law," and not legislators; (3) one can choose to be a haber, "associate," and be particularly concerned with purity, but one need not be one.[20]

Rivkin's conclusions are that from the Tannaitic literature one learns that the Pharisees/perushim-hakamin-soferim were: (1) a scholar class, (2) devoted to the twofold law, (3) actively opposed the Sadducees and (4) would use dramatic means to assert their authority. This picture of the Pharisees is similar to the one Rivkin draws from Josephus (Ant. XIII.297) and the New Testament (Gal. 1:14; Phil. 3:5-6; Mt. 23:2; Mk. 7:5-9).

Rivkin's reconstruction of the history of the Pharisees is based chiefly on Josephus, the only one of our sources that presents a historical account. Rivkin claims that the Pharisaic revolution took place at the time of the Maccabean revolt.[21] Our latest pre-Maccabean source, Ben Sira, is a pro-priestly document with no concept of the twofold law. Our first references to the Pharisees in Josephus are in a description of Jewish sects set in his account of Jonathan the

Maccabee and his account of John Hyrcanus, where the Pharisees were the king's teachers. Therefore, the Pharisees appeared during the period between Ben Sira and John Hyrcanus. Rivkin suggests that the Maccabean revolt provided the changes in the structure of Jewish life that allowed new political religious groups to grow.

What is immediately striking about Rivkin's definition of the Pharisees is what he leaves out. The Pharisees are not a sectarian group primarily concerned with ritual purity. They are a political group with a specific understanding of Jewish tradition, the twofold law. The details of the twofold law are not specified.

Rivkin's understanding of the Pharisees is flawed by his identification of the traditions of the Pharisees with the oral Law.[24] Although the teachings of the Tannaitic Rabbis came to be described as the revealed oral Law, this identification is late fourth century.[25]

Another problem with Rivkin's approach is his tendency to treat the three major sources of information, Josephus, New Testament and Tannatic materials, as if they were internally homogeneous. He does not consider the implications of a more critical approach to the source material to his understanding of the Pharisees.

The image Rivkin uses to describe the Pharisees' authority, "sitting on Moses' seat," comes from the speech against the Pharisees in Mt. 23. The complaint against the Pharisees' authority need not be taken as evidence for their political power. Neusner points out the limited range of issues which Matthew describes as the Pharisees' concerns: tithing, vows to the Temple, prostelytism and table laws.[28] The speech may represent tensions between the concerns of the community behind Matthew and those of the Pharisaic teachers in the post-70 period, as much as, or more so than, a conflict between Jesus and the Pharisees. The extent to which we identify Matthew's concern will help us describe the concerns of the Pharisees he is arguing against.[29]

Rivkin's contribution to an understanding of the Pharisees pushes his lexigraphically sensitive method to its limits. There is no doubt that Josephus describes the Pharisees as a political party and that the Rabbis wielded political power in the post-70 period. They retired from active political life in the latter half of the first century B.C.E. and restricted their concern to "religious" matters. This is more likely due to a decline in Jewish autonomy than to Rivkin's concept of a "Great Compromise" between Salome-Alexandra and the Pharisees. Though Rivkin cannot tell us the details of the Pharisaic traditions, he is correct in seeing the Law (and tradition) as a central element mediating, in a covenantal sense, God's love and the rewards of being in Israel, eternal life.

Rivkin's approach is useful for Jewish-Christian dialogue. He stresses a basic structural system in the three Western religions. By his use of New Testament images and language--for example, "Moses' seat," "God so loved the individual"--he points out the dependence of Christianity upon the matrix of first-century Judaism.

Yet, because of his inability to provide a clear picture of Pharisaic Law, it is difficult to say exactly how Christianity differed. Is the goal of the internalized Law the same as that of the internalized Christ? Is Christianity, for Rivkin, another form of Judaism, or is it a different religion with a different worldview and different goals?

C. Jacob Neusner: "Sanctification and the Power of One's Will"

Jacob Neusner's work on the Pharisees is part of an at-least-twenty-year study of Rabbinic materials, with the concern of providing a description of Judaism represented by the Mishnah. Neusner's own work has undergone a long development, from Talmudic biography, to history, to critical analyses of texts, to, finally, a description of Judaism based on the detailed critical analysis and a study of the sociological interests of the groups in Judaism behind the Mishnah. Along the way, he has retranslated the Mishnah with commentary, translated the Tosefta, translated the Palestinian Talmud and plans to retranslate the Babylonian Talmud. He has produced a school of disciples and has influenced many more through his unending flow of books, articles and essays.[30]

In his book, _Judaism, The Evidence of the Mishnah_, Neusner attempts to summarize his work on Tannaitic sources.[31] The Mishnah, the first of the Tannaitic sources to be edited, represents the needs of three different social groups: (1) a caste--priests, (2) a profession--scribes and (3) a class--householders. The goal of the Mishnaic system was to affirm the ability of humanity to bring order to creation through a process of sanctification. This desire for order is seen in the Mishnah's desire to resolve doubtful situations by a process of even more specific categories. "It is in this method of sorting out things that the Mishnah becomes truly Mishnaic."[32] The areas of the Mishnah's concern are areas of doubt.

Sanctification, the differentiation between the holy and not-holy, that is, the clean and the unclean, forms the central part of this process. It is humans, above all, who have the power to sanctify, to make holy, to bring order.

The Mishnah is the product of humans who rebuilt Judaism as a way of life, dedicated to order, stability and holiness, in an unstable world. The earlier focus of holiness and order, the Temple in Jerusalem, had been destroyed, and the Jews had been defeated in two brutal wars. Yet they built a system in which the holy people, Israel, living in the holy land, the Land of Israel, would find holiness. The center of holiness became the village and the home, not the Temple and the altar.

The power to sanctify was no longer inherent in a holy object, such as the altar, as in biblical times. The Mishnah's theory of holiness is transactional: God and humanity are the agents of sanctification. In the case of agricultural products, God, as the owner of the land, has a claim in its products, and humans must acknowledge God's claim and set aside God's portion. It is humans, however, who sanctify, for they are the ones who designate and separate the produce and acknowledge God's claim.[33]

For Neusner, the greatest problem in understanding the Pharisees is that our major sources have been edited after the fall of Jerusalem in 70 C.E. For Neusner, the fall of Jerusalem marks a watershed in Jewish history. Our sources on the Pharisees all have been shaped in reaction to that event and cannot be relied upon to provide unbiased information for the pre-70 period. They each have their own agenda.

This realization led Neusner to take a highly critical approach to the material. One of his major contributions to the study of Mishnah is his application of higher critical questions to the material in searching for the sources and schools that produced the document. Unlike the Bible, in which variations in style, language and theme help the scholar identify and date different sources within the literature, the Mishnah is a homogeneous book. A distinctive style and language characterizes the whole work.

Being unable to analyze the Mishnah on the basis of stylistic and linguistic variations, Neusner uses attestations, that is, the way the Mishnah attributes sayings to one master or another, to establish the sources of the Mishnah. An attestation provides a terminus ante quem, a point before which a tradition had to be known. That is, the issue discussed was, at least, a concern of the person to whom it is attributed. For Neusner, there are three ways of establishing a date for a Rabbinic tradition: (1) contemporary evidence outside of the Rabbinic literature--such evidence does not exist at present; (2) the date of the final redaction of the material; (3) the internal evidence of the traditions. If the comments of a post-70 master are incidental to a discussion of pre-70 masters, one can assume that the discussion existed before the post-70 master. If his comments are essential to the discussion, then it represents issues of his time and not earlier.

Using this method, Neusner is able to discern three levels in the development of the Mishnah. Each level has its own concerns. The three levels are: (1) Pre-70, before the destruction of Jerusalem: concerns of a holiness sect; (2) between the Wars, 70-125, the masters at Yavneh: concerned with building a vision for all Israel with the center being the home and village, and reform of the Temple cult by lay virtuosi of the law, not priests; (3) after the Wars, 140-200 C.E., the masters at Usha and the final editing by Judah the Prince (c. 200 C.E.): concerned with organization, completion of the Mishnah and establishing its connection with scripture.

The Mishnah does not give us a full picture of the pre-70 masters. From the material that can be attributed to them, we see they had a special interest in laws of purity and agriculture, because these two areas directly affected their table fellowship. They were a group of laity who wanted to act like priests, and priests who wished to extend holiness beyond the bounds of the Temple.

The pre-70 masters were concerned with group-defining activities and rules, that is, meals and marriage. They showed no concern with the activities of the Temple cult. They appear to have no control over Temple worship. For Neusner, the cultic legislation in the Mishnah is a product of reforming tendencies in the Yavneh period after the fall of the Temple.

The Mishnah does not identify this group of masters by name. The only two pre-70 masters who appear both inside and outside of our Rabbinic literature are Gamaliel and Simeon ben Gamaliel in Acts 5:31 and in Josephus, Life 191, respectively. They are identified in those outside sources as Pharisees.

The Mishnah expresses priestly themes of holiness and separation. Even on this early level, however, the Mishnah expresses itself differently than priestly material. It reflects the list-making style of scribes.[34]

Neusner's understanding of the Pharisees and the Judaism of the Mishnah presents a number of important implications to Jewish-Christian dialogue. Most importantly, by stressing the originality of the masters of the Mishnah, he makes room for a Christianity that is not dependent on the immediate ancestor of modern Judaism. Both traditions have their roots in the Judaism of the pre-70 period but developed differently as a result of the pressures upon Judaism that produced the disastrous two revolts against Rome.

Neusner's view of the Pharisees diffuses the polemic seen in the Synoptic Gospels. The conflict between Jesus and the Pharisees is artificial. The Pharisees are straw persons for Jesus to knock down. There is no real conflict, because their goals are different. The goal of the Pharisees and the Mishnaic masters is sanctification, while that of Jesus and his followers is salvation.

Neusner emphasizes that the Mishnah is an heir of biblical Judaism. It has its own agenda, that is, establishing an orderly, stable society based on the sanctification of everyday life. It chose as its scriptural base those parts of the Bible that reflected its concerns, primarily the priestly legislature. He acknowledges that other varieties of Judaism would have different agendas and different choices of scripture. For example, nascent Christianity took salvation as its agenda and chose certain prophetic writings as its scriptural base.[35]

Neusner stresses the social base of Mishnaic Judaism. The Mishnah reflects the needs of the Jewish farmer-landowner in the rural villages of the land of Israel. The corporate, communal life of the Jewish people on their land provides the social state for Mishnaic Judaism. Christianity, at a very early stage, left its rural-village background. It became an urban, Gentile phenomenon.[36]

The two traditions--Mishnaic Judaism and early Christianity--both developed from the matrix that describes Judaism before the fall of Jerusalem. They both, however, build upon different aspects of that matrix and, from an early period, developed in different ways.

D. E. P. Sanders: "Patterns of Religion: Covenantal Nomism Versus Participationist Eschatology"

E. P. Sanders' interest in ancient Judaism comes out of his interest in St. Paul. The goal of his two books, <u>Paul and Palestinian Judaism</u> and <u>Paul, the Law and the Jewish People</u>,[37] is to understand "the basic relationship between Paul's religion and the various forms of Palestinian Judaism as revealed in Palestinian Jewish literature from around 200 B.C.E. to around 200 C.E."[38]

For Sanders, Paul's faith and the Judaism of his time represent two different patterns of religion. A pattern of religion is "the description of how a religion is perceived by its adherents to function."[39] It is not a full description of the daily functioning of the religion, nor is it a theological statement summarizing the faith. It expresses the ways adherents of the religion understand "getting in" and "staying in" their faith. A pattern of religion is similar to soteriology, but it is broader. It is not necessarily "unworldly," and it takes in "the beginning, end, and middle of religious life."[40]

Judaism, Sanders claims, shows the pattern of religion he calls "Convenantal Nomism." Put simply, God established a relationship with Israel by entering into a covenant with it. Individual Israelites/Jews experience God within this covenant by maintaining their membership in the people Israel. As the covenant, which God freely made with Israel, entails rules and regulations, the Israelites/Jews try to fulfill these commandments in response to God's loving gift. If they are unable to fulfill the commandments, they are not excluded from Israel but maintain their good standing by a process called <u>Teshuvah</u>, "repentance," literally "returning."[41]

Sanders describes Paul's religion as "Participationist Eschatology":

> God has sent Christ to be the savior of all, both Jew and Gentile (and has called Paul to be the apostle to the Gentiles); one participates in salvation by becoming one person with Christ, dying with him to sin and sharing the promise of his resurrection; the transformation, however, will not be completed until the Lord returns; meanwhile, one who is in Christ has been freed from the power of sin, . . . and his behavior should be determined by the new situation; since Christ died to save all, all men must have been under the dominion of sin, 'in the flesh' as opposed to being in the Spirit.[42]

Sanders compares Paul to the Judaisms of the 400-year period from 200 B.C.E. to 200 C.E. The first section of <u>Paul and Palestinian Judaism</u> begins with a study of Tannaitic Judaism. Like Rivkin, Sanders draws upon the vast range of materials considered Tannaitic: Mishnah, Tosefta, Tannaitic midrashim and baraitot, Tannaitic material in the Talmud. Sanders treats the material as a group. He is not concerned with issues of date and provenance, for he is looking at the broad picture, the patter of religion presented by the material. His control is the other bodies of Jewish literature: Qumran, the Apocrypha and the Pseudepigrapha. They also present the same pattern of religion.

One of Sanders' major goals is to discredit the view of Judaism as a dry, legalistic faith trapped in a salvation system based on the belief that one earns salvation by performing good deeds. With this goal in mind, he begins his discussion of Tannaitic material with a lengthy criticism of the scholarly champions of such a negative view: F. Weber, Bousset, Schürer, Billerbeck and Bultmann. Basically, they approached Judaism with a theological agenda which led them to see Judaism as the negative image of Christianity.

Sanders feels free to discuss the Tannaitic literature as a whole in part because of the tendency of these scholars to treat the Pharisees and the Tannaitic Rabbis as a group. Billerbeck, for example, calls the works-righteousness he finds in Talmudic literature "Pharisaic soteriology."

Sanders further defends his use of Tannaitic material by arguing that it is a collective literature (after Neusner). The individual's view is not important, and on certain issues there is a consensus.

Although Paul and the Rabbis represent different patterns of religion, neither present systematic theologies. Sanders applies the insight of Max Kaddushin[43]--that Rabbinic thought is organic and that it is coherent but not necessarily a systematic, integrated pattern--to his understanding of Paul and the Rabbis. The coherence lies in an organic complex in which a number of basic concepts interact with one another. Each of the basic concepts is independent. They cannot be derived from the other, yet they are mutually interrelated. They do not stand alone.

This allows for differing interpretations of the same biblical text and historical experiences. Different fundamental concepts come into play in different situations. The fundamental concepts are not related hierarchically or systematically, but organically. Thus, for example, the Rabbis could describe the covenant and the election of Israel as coming about: (1) because it was offered gratuitously for God's name's sake; (2) it was offered to all nations, and only Israel accepted it; (3) it was offered because of the merit of the Patriarchs, the exodus generation or future obedience.

Sanders does not see his approach as a-historical as Kaddushin's, nor are Sanders' concerns as broad as Kaddushin's. Rather, the concept of organic thinking enables Sanders to make use of Rabbinic material as a group.

It also provides Sanders with a key to Paul. Sanders explains Paul's positions on the Law and on the Jewish people, for example, as being attempts to express Paul's conflicting basic convictions. In dealing with the Law, Paul was torn between his belief that Jews and Gentiles were made righteous on the same basis through faith in Christ and that the Law was part of God's plan and is, therefore, valuable. In dealing with the Jewish people, Paul tried to maintain the continuity of God's promises to Israel, even though Jews and Gentiles are saved on the same basis. The tensions in Paul rise out of conflicts between his basic principles.

The basic contribution of Sanders' work is his demonstration of the theological foundation to the negative portrayal of the Pharisees and Rabbinic Judaism by earlier scholars. In addition, Sanders presents Judaism as being essentially different from Pauline Christianity. They both represented different patterns of religion.

In his work on Paul, Sanders argues that Paul did not reject Judaism for personal reasons. Paul turned away from Judaism and offered a different type of religion because of his concern for the salvation of the Gentiles.

Sanders demonstrates that it is possible for Christians to have a positive evaluation of the Judaism of the Pharisees and the Rabbis without detracting from the power and originality of early Christianity. By understanding Paul as a coherent, pragmatic thinker and not a systematic thinker, Sanders is able to allow tensions to remain in Paul's thought. Sanders does not see Paul projecting salvation for Israel apart from Christ. There is only one olive tree, and the condition for being a branch is faith (Rom. 11:23).

Though he holds that his reading of Paul does not provide an adequate basis for a Jewish-Christian dialogue, he personally does not feel bound to Paul's first-century solutions.[45] In light of the continued existence of both the church and the Jewish people, Sanders feels that if Paul were to write today he would continue to find new ways to maintain his basic principles.

With his understanding of Pharisaic and Tannaitic
Judaism as a vital religion living in response to God's
grace, and of Paul as a dynamic, organic thinker,
Sanders shows a way in which both traditions can accept
each other in a positive light as different types of
religion, with different goals and structures.

III. IMPLICATIONS

What recent research shows is that very little is
known with certitude about the Pharisees. The leading
scholars disagree in terms of method and of results.
Different questions lead to different answers. If the
answers are not contradictory, they are certainly not
complementary.

The major contribution of Bowker (Christian) was
collecting the major texts in English translation. His
attempt to differentiate between "Good" Pharisees and
"Bad" Pharisees, to explain the development of
Pharisaism and Jesus' conflict with them, is flawed by
his uncritical approach to the material. One cannot
identify the "Bad" Pharisees of Jesus' time with the
"Bad" Pharisees found in Rabbinic texts 200 years
younger.

Rivkin, Neusner and Sanders approach the material
with a greater sensitivity to the critical problems.
Their results are too divergent to be useful and closely reflect the concerns of the researchers.

Rivkin (Jewish), a professor at the Hebrew Union
College, Cincinatti, Ohio, approaches the problem of
the Pharisees basically as a historian concerned with
the political and economic forces that shape history.
It is not surprising that the image of the Pharisees in
the historian Josephus forms the base for Rivkin's picture of the Pharisees as a political group with a
distinctive ideological agenda.

Neusner (Jewish), a professor at Brown University
in Providence, Rhode Island, comes to the issue of the
Pharisees with the skills of a text critic and the
interests of a social historian. Once again, it is not
surprising that he bases his view of the Pharisees on
his detailed, higher-critical work on the Mishnah. Nor
is it unusual that he attempts to discover the social
groups behind the document by the issues discussed
within it.

Sanders (Christian) is a professor of religious studies at McMaster University, Hamilton, Ontario. His area of study is New Testament. Although he has made a major contribution to the study of early Judaism, his focus is on St. Paul's thought, not on the various forms of ancient Judaism.

With what does all this leave us? In the first place, we have been brought beyond the results of previous scholarship. Neusner and Sanders--and, to a lesser extent, Rivkin--demonstrate that it was faulted by bad method and theological presuppositions. Second, it is clear that we need to go beyond the view of the Pharisees as the "brood of vipers," as religious hypocrites. The question is: where?

We have before us four pictures of the Pharisees: (a) as moderate and extremist members of a popular sect concerned with purity (Bowker); (b) as an active political group dedicated to a view of Jewish Law as twofold, stressing God's love and a resurrection of the dead, with the twofold law linking both of them (Rivkin); (c) as a group of laity who desired to be priests, and priests who wished to extend purity to the whole people, whose concern for group identity focused on table-fellowship, who formed the philosophical roots for the Mishnah's program of sanctification (Neusner); (d) as a religious group that promised individual members future spiritual rewards as long as they were committed to belong to the group and follow its laws as a worshipful response to the God who, in love, gave them (Sanders).

With such a diversity of views, as well as the lack of detailed information provided by any one of these scholars, it is very difficult to develop a picture of the Pharisees useful to interreligious dialogue. Any conclusions about the relationship of Jesus and the Pharisees become very tenuous.

Michael Cook concludes his article, "Jesus and the Pharisees--The Problem as It Stands Today," with the following observations on apparent parallels between Jesus and the Pharisees: "Our knowledge of the historical Jesus is limited. If eschatology is central to Jesus' message, as Schweitzer held, then perhaps apparent parallels are not important, for eschatology is not important in any view of the Pharisees. If it is the case that the eschatological concerns should be ascribed to the early Church and not to Jesus, then the parallels might be important." In any case, similarities such as the parable form, the centrality of the Reign of God and the use of the golden rule may only reflect a common Jewish background.[46] Cook ends with the note that an expertise in both New Testament and Rabbinics is needed to approach the problem.[47]

Yet, some things can be said. Whether or not Jesus was a Pharisee, the movement he started was not Pharisaic. Whatever Paul's claims to have been a Pharisee mean, it is clear that he no longer saw himself as one (Phil. 3:2-7). In the Synoptic Gospels, Jesus is usually in conflict and not in agreement with the Pharisees. They argue about the nature of the Law (central for Rivkin), and about details such as purity, tithing, and Sabbath (central for Neusner). They only seem to agree against the Sadducees on the issue of resurrection (Mt. 22:23-33; Mk. 12:18-27; Lk. 20:27-40; see also Acts 23:6-10). Yet, resurrection is found in other bodies of Jewish literature and need not be seen as a purely Pharisaic doctrine. The support given to the early Christians by Gamaliel, in Acts, is quite limited and not encouraging; the apostles were not killed, but did receive a flogging (Acts 5:33-40).

Christian discipleship is different from Pharisaic discipleship. The apostles, prophets and disciples whom Gerd Theissen[48] describes as wandering charismatics probably have more in common with Honi the Circle Drawer than the students of the sages. Our knowledge of how one became a Rabbinic sage is quite limited. The Mishnah, a document whose form and style betrays the work of Scribes, tells us very little about Scribes themselves. The early Christian movement found its roots among Gentiles in the urban centers of the Roman world, while the Mishnah reflects Jewish life in the rural villages of Palestine.

If Jesus was a Pharisee, his being a Pharisee seems not to be central but incidental to the early church. John Pawlikowski,[49] using the New Testament evidence, suggests seven ways in which Jesus' teachings were a radicalization of Pharisaism:

1. He extended the concept of God as the Father through his personal identification with the Father.

2. He stressed that, at times, the needs of the individual stand in tension with the community's goal of purity and must be fulfilled.

3. He emphasized that a greater sensitivity was needed for the welfare, both physical and spiritual, of the sinners and outcasts, as well as of the amme ha'aretz.

4. He pointed out that wealth, not the evil inclination, was the primary obstacle to discipleship.

5. He linked his person and activities to the Reign of God, beyond the bounds of the Pharisees' thought.

6. He claimed that we are to love, not merely be neutral to, our enemies.

7. He taught ". . . that he had been empowered to forgive sins, and that this power would be imparted to his disciples 'in his name.'"

Even if Pawlikowski is correct in his characterization of Jesus and the Pharisees, one must ask if these extensions of Pharisaism explain the image of Jesus provided by the various New Testament witnesses.

The most striking and radical differences between Jesus and Judaism in this list appear in those cases where Pawlikowski has Jesus personalize an aspect of Pharisaism that was the property of all members of the community: the relationship with the Father, the linkage with God's Reign, and the power to forgive sins.

The Pharisaic tradition is an anonymous, or virtually anonymous, tradition. We do not have individual attestations until after 70 C.E., and even then it is virtually impossible to characterize the sages, much less write a biography. The New Testament rarely mentions Pharisees by name, and those mentioned by Josephus are not connected to the teachings and ideology of the party.

The image of God as Father, the belief in God's Reign and the forgiving of sins are standard Jewish beliefs. They are found in the Hebrew scriptures, in the Jewish noncanonical writings and at Qumran. If Pawlikowski is correct, then the locating of these beliefs in the person of one man, instead of the people or the Temple, may mark the first step in the separation of the Jesus movement from Judaism, including Pharisaism.

In their descriptions of Pharisaism/Tannaitic Judaism, Rivkin, Neusner, and Sanders all indicate how it differed from early Christianity. For Rivkin, in early Christianity Christ replaced the twofold law as the central term of the triad. For Neusner, the Pharisees were concerned with sanctification, while Jesus and his followers were concerned with salvation. For Sanders, at least one early Christian, St. Paul, described a pattern of religion different from that of Judaism.

The implications of modern research on the Pharisees for Jewish-Christian dialogue are:

1. We know very little about the Pharisees and should, therefore, be modest when we discuss and teach the relationship of Jesus and his followers to the Pharisees.

2. What makes Christianity important is that it is not Pharisaism or Tannaitic Judaism. It was not what Jesus had in common with the Pharisees that made an impact on his followers but what they found distinctive in him. Yet it is important to remember that Christianity, as well as Rabbinic Judaism has its roots in first-century Judaism in which the Pharisees played an important role.

3. Pharisaism and Tannaitic Judaism can no longer be described as a dead faith based on works-righteousness. Rather, it provided Jews with living religious experiences and directed their lives to the specific goal of

sanctification, making holiness present and available to all.

4. We should go and study.

NOTES

1 Ellis Rivkin, A Hidden Revolution, The Pharisees' Search for the Kingdom Within (Nashville: Abingdon, 1978).

2 John Bowker, Jesus and the Pharisees (Cambridge: University Press, 1973), provides a collection of the basic texts pertaining to the Pharisees in English translation, pp. 77-179. For a brief summary of problems, see Michael Cook, "Jesus and the Pharisees. The Problem as It Stands Today," Journal of Ecumenical Studies, vol. 15 (Summer, 1978), pp. 441-460.

3 Rosemary Ruether, Faith and Fratricide, The Theological Roots of Anti-Semitism (New York: The Seabury Press, 1974).

4 E. P. Sanders, Paul and Palestinian Judaism (Philadelphia: Fortress Press, 1977). Charlotte Klein, Anti-Judaism in Christian Theology (Philadelphia: Fortress Press, 1978).

5 Nancy Fuchs-Kreimer, "Christian Old Testament Theology: A Time for New Beginnings," Journal of Ecumenical Studies, vol. 18 (Winter, 1981), pp. 76-92, discusses the impact of the evaluation of Judaism on the Old Testament Theology Movement in the United States, 1940-1960. One cannot neatly divide the schools between German and English language. The negative picture of the Pharisees is common in English language scholarship as well. This is seen clearly in Matthew Black's article in the Interpreters Dictionary of the Bible, vol. 3, pp. 774-781, in which he describes Pharisaism as "the immediate ancestors of rabbinical (or normative) Judaism, the largely arid religion of the Jews after the fall of Jerusalem . . .," and as ". . . a sterile religion of codefied tradition . . ." It is to the credit of the editors of the Interpreters Dictionary of the Bible that, in their supplementary volume, the article on Pharisees is by Ellis Rivkin, whose contribution will be discussed in this article.

6 Billerbeck's work is flawed by his view of Judaism, that is, "Pharisaic soteriology," which determined his selection of Rabbinic material for his commentary. "Pharisaic soteriology," briefly, is a system of works-righteousness in which the believer attempted

154

to earn more merits than demerits, to obtain paradise. Scholars, unaware of or unconcerned with Billerbeck's point of view, used the Kommentar as if it were the original source, instead of a useful, although flawed, tool for entering the broad range of Rabbinic literature: Sanders, Paul and Palestinian Judaism, pp. 42-43. For further critique of Billerbeck, see S. Sandmel's classic article, "Parallelomania," Journal of Biblical Literature, vol. 81 (1962), pp. 8-10.

[7] Sanders, Paul and Palestinian Judaism, pp. 33-59. G. F. Moore, "Christian Writers on Judaism," Harvard Theological Review, vol. 14 (1921), pp. 197-254.

[8] For a summary of recent developments, see Philip Culbertson, "Changing Christian Images of the Pharisees," Anglican Theological Review, vol. 64 (1982), pp. 539-561. Also see Leonard Swidler, "Pharisees in Recent Catholic Writing," Horizons, vol. 10 (1983), pp. 267-287. John T. Pawlikowski, "Jesus and the Pharisaic Tradition," in his What Are They Saying about Christian-Jewish Relations? (New York: Paulist Press, 1980). For pertinent, official church statements, see Helga Croner, Stepping Stones to Further Jewish-Christian Relations (London and New York: Stimulus Books, 1977). For a study of Catholic textbooks in the United States, see Eugene Fisher, Faith without Prejudice (New York: Paulist Press, 1977).

[9] Cook, "Jesus and the Pharisees," pp. 442-444.

[10] Jacob Neusner recognizes the implication of the critical study of Rabbinic materials to a reevaluation of Rabbinic thought and Jewish theology in general. In an evaluation of his own work, particularly his translations of Rabbinic materials, he writes: "The sources under study in this book have in general served an other than historical enterprise. They too long have lain in the hands of theologians, who care only for results reached long ago, for the imaginative, the possible, the proposal, the conjecture, and what might be true. We deal with the treasures of the human imagination. The theologians think they hold the key to the strong box, but long ago they threw away the key and thought to leave the treasure inaccessible, as people would listen to what they reported was in the box. All this is now over. The astonishing human achievements of the ancient sages of Israel now lie

open for anyone who wants to see. The keepers of the treasure have been dismissed. For now they too have to meet the standards of rationality, criticism, actuality, disposal, and either show what is in fact the case or shut up" ("Preface," in his Formative Judaism: Religious, Historical and Literary Studies, Third Series, Torah, Pharisees and Rabbis [Chico, CA: Scholars Press, 1983], pp. 3-4).

[11] For a recent attempt and up-to-date bibliography, see A. I. Baumgarten, "The Name of the Pharisees," Journal of Biblical Literature, vol. 102 (1983), pp. 411-428. Baumgarten's position is that a possible meaning of the name Pharisee is "specifier." He bases this on a lexigraphical study of the Hebrew root p-r-š, as well as the use of the word akubeia in the description of Pharisees in Greek sources.

[12] See note 2, above.

[13] Ellis Rivkin's position on the Pharisees appears in A Hidden Revolution (see note 1, above), as well as in a series of articles, the most significant of which include:

(1) "Ben Sira and the Nonexistence of the Synagogue: A Study in Historical Method," Abba Hillel Silver Jubilee Volume, 1963.

(2) "The Pharisaic Revolution," in Moses A. Shulvass, ed., Perspectives in Jewish Learning (Chicago, 1966).

(3) "Prolegomenon," in W.O.E. Oesterly and H. Loewe, Judaism and Christianity, vol. 1 (New York: KTAV Reprint, 1969).

(4) "Pharisaism and the Crises of the Individual in the Graeco-Roman World," Jewish Quarterly Review, vol. 61 (1970-71), pp. 27-52.

(5) "Defining the Pharisees: The Tannaitic Sources," Hebrew Union College Annual, vols. 60-61 (1969-70), pp. 205-249.

(6) The Shaping of Jewish History (New York: Charles Scribner's Sons, 1971).

(7) "Beth Din, Boulé, Sanhedrin: A Tragedy of Errors," Hebrew Union College Annual, vol. 46 (1976), pp. 181-199.

(8) For a concise summary of his positions, see his article on the Pharisees in the Supplementary Volume of the Interpreters Dictionary of the Bible (Nashville: Abingdon, 1976), pp. 657-663.

[14] Rivkin, A Hidden Revolution, p. 293.

[15] Ibid., p. 303.

[16] For a detailed presentation of Rivkin's historiography, see David Ellenson, "Ellis Rivkin and the Problems of Pharisaic History: A Study in Historiography," Journal of the American Academy of Religion, vol. 43 (1975), pp. 787-802.

[17] Rivkin, A Hidden Revolution, p. 161.

[18] Ibid., p. 163.

[19] Ibid., pp. 164-165. The other two texts are T. Sot. 15:11-12 and Pes. 70b.

[20] Ibid., p. 177.

[21] Rivkin acknowledges the contributions his mentor, Solomon Zeitlin, made in the development of the method for his definition of the Pharisees but breaks with him on the historical reconstruction. Zeitlin sees the struggles between the Pharisees and Sadducees based upon the tensions in the immediate post-exilic period. See Solomon Zeitlin, The Rise and Fall of the Judean State I (Philadelphia: Jewish Publication Society, 1962), pp. 178-187. For Rivkin's evaluation of, and debt to, Zeitlin, see: the preface to A Hidden Revolution; and "Solomon Zeitlin's Contribution to the Historiography of the Intertestamenteal Period," Judaism, vol. 14 (1965), pp. 354-367.

[22] Rivkin, A Hidden Revolution, pp. 256-257. See also Rivkin, "Ben Sira and the Nonexistence of the Synagogue," and Rivkin, "Beth Din, Boulé, Sanhedrin," to see how the historical questions concerning the Pharisees impact on other central issues in Jewish History in the Second Temple Period.

[23] Rivkin, A Hidden Revolution, p. 258.

[24] Ellenson, "Ellis Rivkin and the Problems of Pharisaic History," pp. 798-799.

[25] Jacob Neusner, "The Myth of the Two Torahs: A Prolegomenon," in Formative Judaism, pp. 7-11. Neusner's thesis is that the doctrine of the two Torahs developed in the fourth century, as a response to triumphant Christianity.

[26] Rivkin, A Hidden Revolution, p. 80.

[27] Ibid. The title of the seventh chapter is "On the Cathedra of Moses."

[28] Jacob Neusner, From Politics to Piety (Englewood Cliffs, N.J.: Prentice Hall, 1973), pp. 73-78.

[29] The Seat of Moses can refer to the Rabbis in Yavneh after the destruction of the Temple, with whom Matthew's community came into contact. The Lukan version of this speech (Lk. 11:37-54) appears in a different context than that of Matthew's. In Luke, Jesus speaks out against the Pharisees after being accused of negligence in matters of ritual purity. In Matthew, however, Jesus presents his remarks to his disciples after effectively silencing his Pharisaic and Sadducean opponents.

[30] For a bibliography of Jacob Neusner's books, see Neusner, Formative Judaism, pp. 175-183. His basic works on the problem of the Pharisees are: The Rabbinic Traditions about the Pharisees before 70 (Leiden: E. J. Brill, 1971), I. The Masters, II. The Houses, III. Conclusions; and a textbook version, From Politics to Piety.

[31] Jacob Neusner, Judaism, the Evidence of the Mishnah (Chicago: The University of Chicago Press, 1981). For an in-depth review of this work and Neusner's method in general, see Shaye J. D. Cohen, "Jacob Neusner, Mishnah and Counter-Rabbinics, A Review Essay," Conservative Judaism, vol. 37 (1983), pp. 48-63. Cohen shows how Neusner's approach to the study of Mishnah and Tannaitic Judaism differs from George Foot Moore's theological-historical approach and Saul Lieberman's detailed study and comparison of rabbinic texts. Cohen calls Neusner's method "counter-

rabbinics" because of Neusner's desire to turn away from the implicit harmonization of Rabbinic texts in these academically traditional methods. Neusner turns to an approach that treats the Mishnah and other Rabbinic documents as self-standing independent units. For a less forgiving view of this book, see Hyam Maccoby, "Jacob Neusner's Mishnah," Midstream, vol. 30, no. 5 (1984), pp. 24-32.

32 Neusner, Judaism, p. 267.

33 Ibid., p. 130.

34 Ibid., p. 71.

35 Ibid., p. 169.

36 Ibid., p. 255. Wayne Meeks, The First Urban Christians, A Social Description of Pauline Christianity (New Haven: Yale University Press, 1982).

37 Sanders, Paul and Palestinian Judaism; E. P. Sanders, Paul, the Law and the Jewish People (Philadelphia: Fortress Press, 1983).

38 Sanders, Paul and Palestinian Judaism, p. 10.

39 Ibid., p. 17.

40 Ibid., p. 18.

41 Ibid., p. 75.

42 Ibid., p. 549.

43 Ibid., p. 72. See Max Kaddushin, The Rabbinic Mind (New York: Bloch, 1952, 1965, 1972).

44 Sanders, Paul and Palestinian Judaism, pp. 87-101.

45 Sanders, Paul, The Law and the Jewish People, p. 197.

46 Cook, "Jesus and the Pharisees," p. 456.

47 Ibid., p. 458.

[48] Gerd Theissen, Sociology of Early Palestinian Christianity, tr. John Bowden (Philadelphia: Fortress Press, 1978).

[49] For list, see Culbertson, "Changing Christian Images of the Pharisees," p. 555. Pawlikowski's position, stressing the close connections of Jesus to the Pharisees, appears in various articles and in chapters of his books:

(1) "The Pharisees and Christianity," The Bible Today, vol. 8 (October, 1970), pp. 47-53.

(2) "On Renewing the Revolution of the Pharisees: A New Approach to Theology and Politics," Cross Currents, vol. 20 (Fall 1970), pp. 415-434.

(3) Catechetics and Prejudice (New York: Paulist Press, 1973).

(4) Sinai and Calvary: A Meeting of Two Peoples (Beverly Hills, CA: Benziger, 1976).

(5) What Are They Saying about Christian-Jewish Relations? (New York: Paulist Press, 1980).

MODERN JEWISH VIEWS OF JESUS--A SEARCH FOR SELF

by

Alan Mittleman

The eminent Protestant theologian Paul M. van Buren has written that in our time a 180-degree turn in attitude is taking place in the churches.[1] Such a fundamental change has not taken place in Christian life in over 1800 years. The change concerns the Christian theological attitude toward Jews and Judaism. Van Buren does not hesitate to attribute this seismic shift in attitude to the out-workings of the Holy Spirit, for the impetus to reconsider the status and significance of the Jews comes not from the side of religion's cultured despisers--ideology, philosophy and so on--but from profound reflection upon the history of the Jews themselves. This has extraordinary significance, van Buren points out, for it must be remembered that the events through which Christians have found God disclosed to them in the past have been events in precisely this history of the Jews. Thus, the impetus for a radical reconsideration of Judaism has come out of the same movement by which revelation has always been interpreted in Christianity: a profound grappling with the meaning of events located in the history of Israel.

Christians have begun to awaken to the continuity and revelatory significance of Jewish history. They have come to recognize that God has never been absent from it and that in the miraculous passage from the ovens of Auschwitz to the kindergartens of modern Israel evidences of a Heilsgeschichte are to be discerned. Van Buren is confident that this incipient revolution in Christian perspective will result in new theological images of the Jewish people. For, even now, Christian theologians are eradicating the old images which derived from a Marcionism more deep and persistent than any church Father could have imagined.

To imply that the Holy Spirit is at work in this theological revisioning, as van Buren does, is to assess its gravity and implications in a most serious and hopeful way. Is there a movement of comparable gravity taking place on the Jewish side? Could one say that there is a fundamental shift in attitude toward Christianity taking place, such that one could attribute to it the guiding hand of the ruah ha-kodesh, the

161

"Holy Spirit"? Alas, the Holy Spirit has never been generous in dispensing unambiguous criteria by which we might discern its operation. One must puzzle out a definitive answer by one's own lights. What can be done is to marshal some evidence for the assertion that there is an analogous movement taking place on the Jewish side. One can call that movement, in Pinchas Lapide's phrase, "the homecoming of Jesus."

In the writing of Jewish theologians, historians, Bible scholars and literary men and women, Jesus has been--tentatively at least--returning to his ancestral home. For 200 years, beginning with Moses Mendelssohn and his contemporaries, Jewish authors have been overturning the medieval Jewish caricature of Jesus and discovering in him a like-minded Jew. While not symmetrical with the Christian theological reappraisal of Judaism, there is a certain similarity. It is, simply, that the Jewish rediscovery of Jesus--like the Christian reappraisal of Judaism--is rooted in a new appreciation of Jewish history. The Jewish rediscovery of Jesus is one result of a very energetic modern Jewish curiosity about the long-neglected diversity of the Jewish past. It represents a desire to discover the complexity of the classical <u>Glaubensgeschichte</u> in order to renew and reinvent the faith of the present. Whether such a phenomenon is inspired by the Holy Spirit remains chronically unclear, but that the Jews have a creative obsession with the richness of their history is an incontrovertible fact. The "homecoming of Jesus," therefore, is an aspect of the modern Jew's act of historically oriented self-discovery, or of self-recovery. It is an aspect of the modern Jew's search for essence and definition.

Although both the Christian rediscovery of Judaism and the Jewish "homeocming of Jesus" derive from a new attentiveness to Jewish history, there is a significant asymmetry between the two. Put simply, in order to make sense of themselves theologically, Christians must make some mention of Judaism, but Jews need not advert to either Christianity or Jesus for their sense-making. No theological necessity compels Jews to speak of Jesus. But, Marcion notwithstanding, the church cannot speak of itself without some talk about the Jews. For 1800 years, the church's way of speaking about the Jews was to speak against them and to convince itself that the Jews were abandoned by God and that their history had come to an end, as the old scholarly designation "<u>Spätjudentum</u>" implies with such twisted eloquence.

Today the church is learning to speak _for_ the Jews, opening itself to the redemptive continuity of Jewish history. Theologically, there is a vast difference between these two ways of speaking, but logically there is no difference. To speak of itself, the church must say _something_ about the Jews.

For Jews, no such relationship of logical-theological dependence exists. Their own covenant with God, never abrogated, endures in "logical isolation" from God's dealings with other peoples. But of course those dealings are not without interest. A Jew might venture to understand, as Franz Rosenzweig did, the shape and meaning of God's positive involvement with others. One could assert that it is parochial for a Jew not to grapple with the acts of God outside of God's relationship with the Jewish people. Certainly the prophets and the rabbis were keenly interested in the fate of the other peoples. One must hope that the unbroken tradition of benevolent universalism in Judaism will deepen in our day. The fundamental fact remains, however, that God's dealings with Israel and Israel's love affair with God are the central foci of Jewish faith.

To qualify this rather harsh judgment, it is true that from a historical point of view Jews must speak of Christianity in order to understand some of the character of their own tradition and of their self-definition. One can think here of the net effects on the Jewish psyche of centuries of minority existences within a generally hostile European Christendom. No Jew believes that the neo-pagan persecutions of the Holocaust could have occurred without centuries of Christian hatred and contempt. Thus, Christianity is always a datum, and most often a negative one, in historical Jewish consciousness.

Christianity is even a factor in the purely religious life of the Jews. The way that the Jews interpret scripture, for example, is shaped in part by the existence of a rival hermeneutic tradition. Rashi, the premier commentator, carries on a constant polemic against Christian allegory in his standard biblical commentary. To this day, Orthodox Jews do not learn Torah without Rashi's guiding hand showing them the way. The dominance of the Oral Tradition as a whole in Judaism has something to do with the recognition that non-Jews have indeed appropriated the scripture, but God has reserved its correct interpretation, the _torah_ she ba'al peh, for the Jews alone. One can also make reference to the elaboration of the dietary laws--the system of kashrut--the complexity of which owes something to an "official" policy of discouraging Jewish table fellowship with non-Jews. All of these practices, and the intellectual and affective cast of mind against which they had their life, were influenced by the presence of a hostile, Christian "other."[2] That historical Christianity influenced Judaism and the Jews in numerous ways is an incontestable and important point for Jewish historical consciousness, but for the reasons outlined above it does not at all bear on the inner logic of Jewish faith. Christianity is therefore factorial but not foundational to Jewish self-awareness and self-definition, while it is certain that Judaism is both factorial and foundational to Christian self-definition.

Jews need not speak of Christianity to get at their own essence, nor must they speak about Jesus. What is novel in the modern Jewish situation is that they choose to do so. In late antiquity and in medieval times, the issue of Jesus was forced upon Jews who had become unwilling participants in a dangerous confrontation. The garbled references to Jesus in the rabbinic literature, as well as the fictional medieval biography of Jesus, Toldot Yeshu, are polemical in intent. The latter is a good deal more contemptuous than the former insofar as the challenge to Jewish survival was much more formidable in the thirteenth century than in the sixth: Justin's "Dialogue with Trypho" was not Pablo Christiani's "dialogue" with Nachmanides. Nonetheless, all pre-modern writings on Jesus fall along a continuum of resentment with a similar, underlying apologetic intention. It is perhaps only in a handful of talmudic quotations where an attitude approaching dispassion can be found.[3]

Given the available forms of historiography in pre-modern eras, Jews could hardly have arrived at a sympathetic or empathetic understanding of Jesus. Like Christians, they saw Jesus as the founder of a new religion. Insofar as "Jesus' religion" grew hostile to Judaism, Jesus himself was held responsible for the errors and malice held to be features of the Christian faith. This tendency was spurred in part by the rabbinic practice of attributing responsibility for the behavior of the disciples to the teaching of the master. In the medieval Jewish mind, Jesus was a renegade rabbi whose torah was either tragically misguided or deliberately vindictive. The punishment which medieval Jews imagined was meted out to Jesus in Gehenna fit the crimes his followers committed. Jesus and the Christian church were inseparably and reciprocally related in the medieval Jewish mind.

Now one of the novel and important features of modern Jewish writing on Jesus is precisely the tendency to disentangle him from the Christian tradition. Owing to modern assumptions about the development and historicity of religious tradition, it is possible to have a positive appraisal of Jesus and a critical, even negative, appraisal of Christianity. This has been the case with key Jewish thinkers, for example, Heinrich Graetz, Leo Baeck and Martin Buber. Buber's Two Types of Faith is a good example. He understands Jesus as an "elder brother" and teacher, all the while criticizing Christianity as a less authentic form of faith than the one lived by its Lord. Leo Baeck provides a similar case. A sympathetic assessment of Jesus emerges in his writings, while a harsh assessment of Christianity, found in such essays as Romantic Religion (burned by the Gestapo), is also to be found. Although Jesus has found a homecoming among his compatriots, the church gathered in his name and often does remain foreign. It ought to be perfectly clear then that the Jewish interest in Jesus has little to do with a desire to convert to Christianity. On the contrary, it has everything to do with a desire to discover the spirit of Judaism and to shape a faith for the present in light of the hidden potentialities of the past.

The "homecoming of Jesus" is a phenomenon within the modern Jewish process of self-definition and renewal. But, of course, the "Jewish Jesus" is not there to be rediscovered simpliciter. He inheres in the Christian canon and tradition. The question then is: How has Christian thinking about Jesus influenced Jews in their thinking? What factors within the Christian Umwelt have rendered possible the Jewish "seismic shift" in attitude? Specifically, how has it come about that thinkers such as Mendelssohn, Graetz, Geiger, Montefiore and Klausner, and more recently Buber, Ben-Chorin, Flusser and Lapide have been moved to such a positive engagement with the person of Jesus? What are the implications for a Judaism whose thinkers have "welcomed Jesus home"? This latter question suggests that the homecoming of Jesus is basically a domestic matter with domestic implications. The other questions remind us that the household, however, is set

165

in the midst of a Christian landscape. To continue to employ this metaphor, what changes have taken place in the landscape, and what changes have taken place at home?

First, the landscape. Jewish life has undergone a series of great upheavals in the past 200 years. In the late eighteenth and early nineteenth centuries, Jews in the West experienced the Enlightenment and their civic emancipation. In our own century, Jews have experienced both a persecution of historically unprecedented ferocity and the rebirth of a state in their homeland: <u>bayit shelishi</u>, the third Jewish commonwealth. Furthermore, Jews in America have had their own experience of a historical novum: greater acceptance, security and positive exposure to other religious cultures than ever before in their history. Were it not for these great dislocations and alterations in the patterns of Jewish communal and intellectual life, there certainly would have been no Jewish rediscovery of Jesus.

By way of example, Moses Mendelssohn represents a transitional figure for both Jewish writing on Jesus and correlative Jewish struggle for self-definition in modernity. Mendelssohn was a giant of the German Enlightenment, living from 1729 to 1786. He discerned an attitude of greater acceptance among the Christians to Jews like himself who learned the ways of German culture. The possibility of friendship with a man such as Lessing or of friendly competition with Kant signaled a social environment that seemed capable of fundamental change. The <u>Aufklärung</u> and its skepticism toward revealed religion and traditional attitudes provided a neutral meeting place for both the Christian and the Jewish enlightened. A new ideal of humanity and a rationalistic, deist spirituality provided alternatives to the traditional anthropologies and faith-disciplines of Judaism and Christianity. Imbued with this spirit and set on educating the Jews to be prepared for the emancipation which a beneficent Providence would soon effect, Mendelssohn sought to introduce intellectual and cultural reforms in Jewish life. Mendelssohn originated a movement of Jewish enlightenment of "<u>Haskalah</u>" which paralleled the Enlightenment fascination with moral <u>Bildung</u>. It emphasized virtue and moral perfection, as did its German parent, but it was also remedial. It sought to educate Jews in the necessary elements of German culture so as both to participate in that culture and to renew their own culture under the guidance of contemporary norms.

Given a climate of Christian tolerance and rationalism and his own agenda for Jewish renewal, Mendelssohn was able to reject the view of Jesus which prevailed in the popular Jewish mind and assert that Jesus was good man, whose teaching was congruent with that of his rabbinic contemporaries. Jesus was misunderstood by his contemporaries and his Christian followers, but his intentions--the chief criterion of virtue for Enlightenment thinkers--were good.[4] The context of this affirmation of a Jewish Jesus was Mendelssohn's unwelcome conversation with Johann Caspar Lavater. The latter challenged the Jewish philosopher to explain why he had not accepted the divinity of Christ and acquiesced to the superiority of Christianity. The ensuing correspondence transported Mendelssohn back to a world which he hoped had forever vanished.

Mendelssohn was forced to play the role of the disputant in order to uphold the honor of Judaism. Following medieval polemics, he argued with Lavater that Judaism was morally superior to Christianity insofar as it was not offensive to reason, nor did it compel its followers to coerce others to its tenets.[5] Here emerges a pattern destined to be repeated in modern Jewish thought: a reclamation of Jesus as a Jew coupled with a negative appraisal of Christianity.

With Mendelssohn's modest Jesus, the rabbi of Nazareth once again assumed a place among the Jewish teachers of the classical age that is both benign and sympathetic. Mendelssohn was not exactly alone in his reconsideration; his traditional colleague Rabbi Jacob Emden also endorsed a fair and sober view of Jesus. In Emden's case, Christanity assumed a fairly benign profile as well.[6] It is clear that Emden wanted to stimulate friendly contacts between Jews and Christians as did Mendelssohn and that this motive was at the bottom of his positive stance toward Jesus and Christianity. Emden, however, opposed the Enlightenment and its Jewish response, Haskalah. He anticipated a more secure and congenial social environment and wrote of Christianity only with the aim of facilitating the Jew's acceptance of what seemed to him only a renewal of an essentially medieval tolerance. Emden envisioned an amelioration of the old world, while Mendelssohn was out to create a new world--and a new Jewish humanity.

Consequently, it is Mendelssohn and not Emden who must be credited with initiating the "homecoming" of Jesus. If it is clear what Mendelssohn's "landscape" looked like, it ought also to be clear how the household of his faith appears as well: In an Enlightenment religion of reason and virtue, a modest Jewish teacher of noble ethics appears. Jesus has become one of the first Aufklärungsmenschen.

The Christian landscape of the Enlightenment changed in the early nineteenth century, and with it came a change in the German Jewish household. The Enlightenment, following earlier patterns of rationalism, emphasized a rather disembodied concept of reason as the most compelling and characteristic feature of humanity. With the nineteenth century, the concept of history and of humans as creatures tied to a progress of development in history became dominant. The growth of a greater awareness of the historicity of tradition, indeed of Being, provided an alternative for a Christian faith hard-pressed by the abstract universalism of Enlightenment religion. Beginning with Reimarus, there was a new fascination with the Jesus of history, with Jesus the human, retrieved from under the glittering medieval icon of Jesus the Christ. Historically oriented research on the career of Jesus (Lebens Jesu Forschung) opened up a line of defense for scholarly Christians whose faith had been shaken by Enlightenment rationalism. Research into the life of Jesus was not only a rearguard action against a corrosive rationalism, but it was also a reflex of that rationalism, and it was as upsetting to the traditionalists as the Enlightenment had been. The Christian rediscovery of Jesus as a historical Jewish man in first-century Palestine was hardly a source of solace to orthodox Christians.

The new affirmation of history--the redemption of history from a nondevelopmental, a-historical consciousness--initiated a revolution in perspective among Mendelssohn's Jewish heirs. The great work of Isaac Marcus Jost, Heinrich Graetz, Abraham Geiger, and Leopold Zunz generated a Wissenschaft des Judentums which still remains a chief outlet of Jewish creativity, as well as an intellectual criterion for theological coherence. The Jewish discovery of historicity did more to topple the traditional mythos of a definitive Sinaitic revelation than did any other factor. Geiger's program of religious reform and Frankel's conservative approach, the two main sources of the current

Jewish denominational picture, were both based on a contemporary fascination with history. The Wissenschaftler sought to rethink, if not to say remake, traditional, Rabbinic Judaism in light of a developmental model of Jewish law and of a more catholic appreciation of the diversity of the Jewish past. From the new historical point of view, orthodoxy became another heterodoxy.

It is in this context that the nineteenth-century recovery of Jesus as a Jew takes place. Graetz provides a good example.[7] Graetz was sympathetic to Jesus and again--quite typically--hostile to Christianity. For Graetz, Jesus was an Essene who was extremely strict in his practice of the Law. He was influenced by John the Baptist who was also an Essene. Graetz believed that these men were Essenes because of the latters' emphasis on immersion--shared by John--and their renunciation of marriage and worldliness--shared by Jesus. The content of Jesus' preaching was rachmanut, compassion and teshuvah, return to God. He was beloved by the disenfranchised to whom he ministered and was of a piece with his contemporaries. Abraham Geiger found a similar figure to that of Graetz's Jesus, except that for him Jesus was a Pharisee, albeit with a Galilean coloring. For both Geiger and Graetz, Jesus was a Jew who was badly misunderstood by his followers. First, Paul distorted his person and message, then his non-Jewish disciples followed Paul's lead. As with Mendelssohn, Jesus had not only returned to Judaism but had definitively parted company with Christianity.

If Mendelssohn can be said to have rearranged the furniture in the Jewish household and to have found room for Jesus in the newly ordered interior, the Wissenschaftler may be thought of as having discovered many unused wings and closets of the home. Graetz embarked on a project of rehabilitating a complex Jewish history which could not help but change one's estimation of the Jewish present. A world in which Essenes and Sadducees became living protagonists in a dialogue about the nature of the tradition--rather than one-dimensional heretics against a faith pre-packaged at Sinai--became a world in which new sense could be made of Jesus. Jesus could reassume a place in Jewish tradition, because many rooms were discovered to constitute the Father's mansion.

Since the pioneering days of _Wissenschaft des Judentums_, much has happened to affect the appraisal of Jesus by Jewish scholars reared in its tradition. In addition to the vast changes in Jewish social life and the "alpine events" of history mentioned above, the methods and the possibilities of _Wissenschaft_ have changed. Scholars are much more critical of the limits of their sources than the early modern historians were. One effect of this critical hermeneutic perspective was a widespread despair of reconstructing the historical Jesus out of documentary evidence that was no longer held to be historically reliable. Curiously, Jews have seemed to be more optimistic about retrieving the historical Jesus than Christians have been. Scholars such as David Flusser have kept aloft the torch of _Lebens Jesu Forschung_ in an age of doubt.

More to the point, the tasks of the Jewish thinker have become more complex in the post-emancipation, post-Enlightenment--post-modern--world. In the world of the twentieth century, the world of Auschwitz and Israel, of America and of interreligious dialogue, the problem of Jewish self-definition is, if no more insistent, more ramified. Contemporary Jews have a larger frame of reference than their early modern counterparts had. They not only have to deal with the more critical intellectual standards of their age, but they also have to deal with much more complicated conditions for Jewish survival. Both an extraordinary degree of freedom in some societies and terrible new forms of discrimination and oppression in others pose uniquely modern challenges. Furthermore, the contemporary Jewish thinker must wrestle with the Jewish experience in the land of Israel. For the first time in two millennia, Jews exist in a society as a majority. The full range of implications of this astonishing fact has yet to be adequately conceptualized.

For all of these reasons, the more recent Jewish reclamation of Jesus is more radical, more problematical than its nineteenth-century predecessors. A good example of this greater depth of engagement is found in the liberal British scholar, C. G. Montefiore. Montefiore continued in the tradition of Reform Judaism espoused by Geiger, but, owing to the high level of acculturation of twentieth-century British Jewry, he was able to arrive at a far more extensive reappraisal. Reflecting that acculturation and writing before the horrors of the Second World War, Montefiore was quite

170

optimistic about the progress of liberal ideals. His Jesus and his Judaism reflect this faith.

Montefiore was a careful scholar, and, unlike his many liberal predecessors who wrote on the Jewish Jesus, he was fully conversant with Protestant biblical scholarship. In his Synoptic Gospels (1909), Rabbinic Literature and Gospel Teaching (1930) and What a Jew Thinks about Jesus (1935), Montefiore confessed his great appreciation for Jesus. Jesus resembled the prophets in intensity and depth. He exceeded the religiosity and insight of the rabbinic sages and gave Jewish tradition its purest articulation. Jesus correctly perceived the dangers of legalism and self-righteousness to which a fixation on the ceremonial law leads and opposed that law with a prophetic critique. Liberal Jews ought to see in Jesus one of their own and reclaim him as a true teacher of the true Jewish way.[8] Indeed, the American Reform leader, Stephen Wise, heeded Montefiore's call in 1925 and preached a sermon espousing these views. The sermon aroused consternation among the Jewish masses, and caused a memorable scandal.

As a leader of the Reform movement, Montefiore saw Judaism as a universalistic faith, the essence of which lay in ethical monotheism. Not surprisingly, this was the faith Jesus pursued with prophetic passion. Montefiore's call for a Jewish reclamation of this Jesus, rooted though it was in the secure, assimilated world of a stratum of British Jewry, should not be construed as an obsequious gesture. It was an ingenuous and serious affirmation of faith. It represents one pole of modern Jewish self-definition. Although somewhat discredited by the consequences of the Holocaust and the reality of the Jewish state, Montefiore's Reform universalism is not witout a constituency today.

One of the significant debates in modern Jewish thought is precisely between this universalistic orientation and the particularist position represented by Zionism. Reflecting this split, Ahad ha-Am, the Hebrew essayist, strongly attacked Montefiore. Ahad ha-Am argued that any appreciation of Jesus by a Jew necessarily indicates a fatal loss of essence. Reconsideration can only mean alienation from Jewish consciousness, estrangement from Jewish substance, and a total effacement of differences. Not content with psychological remarks and sociological predictions, Ahad ha-Am argued against Jesus' teaching and the

171

ethics of the Gospels and attempted to defeat Montefiore on his own ground.[9] One need not be convinced by Ahad ha-Am's polemics or conclusions to acquiesce in one point in his analysis: Montefiore represents an extreme Reform position. Generations of successful acculturation allowed Montefiore and other British Jews a feeling of near-complete identity with their Christian peers that was only an illusion elsewhere. Montefiore's project of Jewish recovery of Jesus derived from and sought to enhance that process of acculturation. By so doing, he hoped to purify a viable, modern Jewish faith.

Ahad ha-Am's perspective was further explicated by Joseph Klausner, who wrote a lengthy Hebrew volume on Jesus--Jesus of Nazareth (1922). Klausner's treatment arises as much from the internal Jewish debate as does Montefiore's, whom Klausner attacks with the same vigor as did his teacher. If Montefiore's Jesus is the ideal Reform Jew, Klausner's Jesus is the perfect foil for Zionism: Jesus becomes everything which a modern Jew should avoid. Klausner, in essence, accepts Montefiore's Jesus and then elaborates reasons to reject such a conception of Jewish existence. Klausner sees in Jesus an observant, although rather lax, Pharisee. He argued against other Pharisees as an insider. What distinguishes him most crucially from his contemporaries was an exaggerated emphasis on individuality over and against group loyalty. Jesus took Pharisaic ethics to an extreme: he emphasized inner transformation and the immanence of the Reign. He believed himself to be the Messiah and spoke in his own name. By so doing, Jesus upset Judaism's delicate balance between the individual and the community. He stressed the solitary individual's relationship with God and severed the nexus between God and people. Jesus failed to gain widespread acceptance among the Jewish people precisely because they were instinctively wary of his anti-collectivist Weltanschauung. The religious foundation which Jesus laid was too narrow to sustain a people.

Klausner's analysis is clearly an attack on Reform Judaism from a post-religious, Zionist point of view. The individualistic, denationalized teacher of ethics is a stand-in for Reform Judaism. Ahad ha-Am and Klausner counterpose the particularist, Zionist definition of Jewish identity against the universalistic one. Jesus has become a symbol in their debate for both the ideal identity of the modern Jew and that which signi-

fies the modern Jew's self-alienation. But this opposition is, after all, something of a false dilemma. As
suggested earlier, Judaism has always been a particu-
larism with a universal horizon. This seeming paradox
fully informs the work of another follower of Ahad
ha-Am, Martin Buber. In Buber, Jesus the Jew becomes
both a universal man of faith and a particularly Jewish
hero.

Buber exceeds both Ahad ha-Am and Klausner by
arriving at a more intense religious conception of
Zionism. Buber's problem, by the time he had written
Two Types of Faith, was to find models of Jewish
existence buried in the past which could be relived in
the Jewish state of the present. Buber discerned a
"subterranean history" of authentic Jewish being, a
sequence of meetings between humanity and God that ran
counter to the official history of established religious forms. The prophets, Jesus, and the early
Hasidim had experienced an I-Thou encounter with the
Eternal Thou. They lived in terms of emunah, a total
commitment of being to God. For Buber, the possibility
of authentic Jewish existence rests upon the reemer-
gence of this subterranean counter-history. The Jewish
community must become the place where humanity meets
God again. The great figures in the counter-history of
the past thus become contemporary exemplars of the
I-Thou encounter. Jesus, whom Buber called his "elder
brother," becomes both an ideal person of faith in a
universalistic sense and a model for the Jewish collec-
tivity to follow. Albeit in a unique and deeper way,
Buber joins the concerns of Montefiore and of Klausner.
Jesus returns home as an ever--present hero of the
Jewish search for self in the presence of God. Modern
Jews could do no better than to regain Jesus' faith.

This universal-religious and particularist-Jewish
Jesus emerges with great nuance in the works of two
students of Buber's way, Shalom Ben-Chorin and Pinchas
Lapide. They both build on Buber's religious insights
and biblical-humanist orientation while deepening the
engagement with contemporary New Testament scholarship.
Additionally, both write in a climate of greatly
enhanced interreligious dialogue and therefore are much
more positive toward Christianity than any of their
scholarly predecessors.

While Ben-Chorin and Lapide have both been active
in Germany, the reality of the State of Israel underlies their works. What is especially interesting about

Jesus is that he is a _sabra_, a native "Israeli" Jew. Jesus' personal religiosity, while sharing much in common with the emerging rabbinic movement, represents one of the indigenous possibilities of "Israeli" spiritual life. Jesus' pristine spirituality, unencumbered by centuries of _halachot_ innovated in the Diaspora, suggests a direction for a new Jewish religiosity in the Land of Israel to follow.

While Ben-Chorin's and Lapide's work border on the technical and must be judged by New Testament scholars, it is also clear that they have made a great impression on the German Christian public. Learned Jewish interest in Jesus itself evokes interest in Jews and Judaism. Ben-Chorin and Lapide reflect the post-war Jewish concern for improving Jewish-Christian relations as a means for enhancing Jewish survival. Again, the "homecoming of Jesus" occurs within the framework of Jewish concerns. The homecoming is understood to be a means of strengthening, while rebuilding, the household.

These few examples of more recent Jewish writers on Jesus make clear that Jesus has come home to a different house in a very different landscape from that of his initial, early modern homecoming. The reasons remain the same, however. The modern Jew is searching for her or himself amid the inherited forms of the past and the difficult terrain of the present. Jesus, though subject to innumerable metamorphoses, has been invited to be a companion on the way. Before the modern era, Jesus was a shadow which followed the Jews against their wills. In more recent times, Jesus has been invited to join in the journey.

Is there anything in this Jewish Jesus for Christians to observe or appreciate? Buber and others have suggested that Jews know Jesus in a different way than do Christians, in a more familial way, and that Christians can learn this form of intimacy from Jews. Must one not believe that "blood" conveys knowledge in order to agree with this assessment? Barring that difficult and perhaps objectionable notion, and agreeing with Schweitzer that all who search for the historical Jesus are likely to remake him in their own image, it would seem that what Christians can learn from the Jews who write of Jesus is how Jews struggle to understand themselves. If the fascination with the rabbi from Nazareth is indeed a medium for self-encounter and discovery as we have argued here, then perhaps Christians

174

may profit from observing this Jewish spiritual quest. For it may very well be that that quest for Jewish self-understanding and essence empowered the soul of the one whom the church calls Lord.

NOTES

[1] Paul M. van Buren, "Theological Education for the Church's Relation to the Jewish People," *Journal of Ecumenical Studies*, vol. 23 (Winter, 1984), p. 490.

[2] Cf. Jacob Katz, *Exclusiveness and Tolerance* (New York: Schocken Books, 1961).

[3] Jacob Z. Lauterbach, "Jesus in the Talmud," in his *Rabbinic Essays* (New York: Ktav Publishing House, 1971).

[4] Hans Joachim Schoeps, *The Jewish-Christian Argument* (London: Faber and Faber, 1963), ch. 6.

[5] Katz, *Exclusiveness*, p. 172.

[6] Ibid., p. 167. Cf. also Harvey Falk, "Rabbi Jacob Emden's Views on Christianity," *Journal of Ecumenical Studies*, vol. 19 (Winter, 1982), pp. 105-111.

[7] Samuel Sandmel, *We Jews and Jesus* (New York: Oxford University Press, 1973), pp. 61-66.

[8] Thomas Walker, *Jewish Views of Jesus* (New York: Macmillan Co., 1931), pp. 50-65.

[9] Ahad ha-Am, "Judaism and the Gospels," in Hans Kohn, ed., *Nationalism and the Jewish Ethic* (New York: Schocken Books, 1962).

CONTRIBUTORS

Leonard Swidler (Catholic), author of over 100 articles and author or editor of over 25 books, is co-founder and Editor of the Journal of Ecumenical Studies. Since 1966 he has been Professor of Catholic Thought and Interreligious Dialogue at Temple University's Religion Department.

Lester Dean (Jewish) has taught religious studies and Bible ("Old" and New Testament) at Temple University for several years while completing his graduate studies in the Religion Department. He is now in the final stages of his dissertation on a Jewish understanding of Pauline thought.

Lewis John Eron (Jewish), ordained Rabbi at the Reconstructionist Rabbinical College in 1981, served as a pulpit rabbi since then until his present appointment as the Executive Director of the Reconstructionist Rabbinical Association. He received his Ph.D. from the Religion Department, Temple University, in 1987.

Johannes Hildebrandt (Lutheran), born in East Prussia, did his theological studies in West and East Berlin 1956-62, when he was ordained pastor. From 1965 to 1969 he was Tutor for Old Testament at the Sprachenkonvikt and since 1969 has been pastor of the Sophienkirche, both in East Berlin.

Alan L. Mittleman (Jewish), ordained Rabbi at the Reconstructionist Rabbinical College in 1981, served as pulpit rabbi several years until joining the national staff of the American Jewish Committee in the area of interreligious affairs. He received his Ph.D. from the Religion Department, Temple University in 1984.

Stefan Schreiner (Lutheran) studied theology and Islamics, earning a Th.D. (1974) in Halle-Wittenberg, and is at present Assistant Lecturer in Hebrew and Old Testament Studies at the Theological Faculty of Humboldt University (East Berlin). He has published numerous books and articles on biblical and qur'anic exegesis, Jewish history, and Jewish-Christian dialogue.

Werner Vogler (Lutheran) studied theology in Leipzig from 1956 to 1960, was ordained pastor in 1962 and served as such until 1969 when he became Dozent for New Testament at the Protestant Theological Seminar Leipzig, where he continues to teach. He received his Th.D. from the University of Greifswald in 1978.